Excellent English 2
Language Skills for Success

Jan Forstrom
Mari Vargo

Marta Pitt
Shirley Velasco

Wookbook by Laurie Blass

Excellent English Workbook 2

Published by McGraw-Hill ESL/ELT, a business unit of The McGraw-Hill Companies, Inc.1221 Avenue of the Americas, New York, NY 10020. Copyright © 2008 by The McGraw-Hill Companies, Inc. All rights reserved. No part of this publication may be reproduced or distributed in any form or by any means, or stored in a database or retrieval system, without the prior written consent of The McGraw-Hill Companies, Inc., including, but not limited to, any network or other electronic storage or transmission, or broadcast for distance learning.

Printed in the United States of America.

ISBN 13: 978-0-07-719766-7 (Workbook)
ISBN 10: 0-07-719766-6
6 7 8 9 10 QVS/QVS 17 16 15 14

Series editor: Nancy Jordan
Developmental editor: Angela Castro
Cover designer: Witz End Design
Interior designer: NETS
Compositor: NETS

Illustrators: Punto 5, Silvia Plata, Ismael Vázquez Sánchez and Carlos Mendoza Alemán

Photo credits:
Page 8: CORBIS, Digital Vision/ Getty Images, Amos Morgan/Getty Images, BananaStock, Ltd, Royalty-Free/CORBIS, Joshua Ets-Hokin; **Page 28** Randy Faris/CORBIS, Thinkstock Images/ Jupiterimages; **Page 31** BananaStock/JupiterImages; **Page 51:** Ryan McVay/Getty Images; **Page 65:** Royalty-Free/ CORBIS, **Page 79:** Stockbyte/Punchstock Images, Getty Images, **Page 83:** Dennis Wise/Getty Images, C Squared Studios/Getty Images, Michael Matisse/Getty Images; **Page 91:** Royalty-Free/CORBIS, Brand X Pictures/Punchstock, Getty Images, Royalty-Free/CORBIS, Doug Menuez/Getty Images, Royalty-Free/ CORBIS, Digital Vision/Getty Images, **Page 93:** Jack Hollingsworth/Getty Images, **Page 104:** Goodshoot/ PunchStock, PhotoLink/Getty Images, John A. Rizzo/Getty Images, Mitch Hrdlicka/Getty Images, Ingram Publishing/Alamy, Image Source/CORBIS, Ingram Publishing/Alamy, JupiterImages/ImageSource, PhotoLink/Getty Images, Royalty-Free/CORBIS, Comstock/PunchStock, Burke/Triolo/Getty Images, **Page 107:** PhotoAlto/PictureQuest, **Page 121:** Stockbyte/PunchStock, Royalty-Free/CORBIS, trbfoto/Brand X Pictures/ JupiterImages, Stockbyte/PunchStock, Nick Koudis/Getty Images, Creatas/ PunchStock, **Page 124:** Photodisc/Getty Images, **Page 135:** Nick Clements/Getty Images, Keith Brofsky/ Getty Images, Thinkstock/JupiterImages, **Page 147:** RubberBall Productions/ Getty Images, Doug Menuez/Getty Images, Royalty-Free/CORBIS, Royalty-Free/CORBIS, PunchStock, **Page 148:** BananaStock Ltd., **Page 149:** BananaStock Ltd., Royalty-Free/CORBIS, **Page 161:** Comstock Images/ JupiterImages, Getty Images, Eyewire (Photodisc)/ PunchStock, Pixland/PunchStock, Digital Vision/PunchStock, Lawrence Manning/CORBIS, **Page 163:** Steve Mason/Getty Images, Dynamic Graphics/ PictureQuest, **Page 164:** Stockbyte/PunchStock, Stockbyte/PunchStock, Stockbyte/PunchStock, PhotoLink/Getty Images, Royalty-Free/CORBIS

Cover photo:
Hand: Getty
Dentist: Corbis
Smiling family: Corbis
Business woman: Corbis
Graduate: Corbis

To the Teacher

PROGRAM OVERVIEW

> **Excellent English: Language Skills for Success** equips students with the grammar and skills they need to access community resources while developing the foundation for long-term career and academic success.

Excellent English is a four-level, grammar-oriented series for English learners featuring a *Grammar Picture Dictionary* approach to vocabulary building and grammar acquisition. An accessible and predictable sequence of lessons in each unit systematically builds language and math skills around life-skill topics. *Excellent English* is tightly correlated to all of the major standards for adult instruction.

- CASAS (the Comprehensive Adult Student Assessment Systems)
- Los Angeles Unified School District's Competency-Based Education (CBE) Course Outlines
- Florida Adult ESOL Syllabi
- EFF (Equipped for the Future) Content Standards
- SCANS (Secretary's Commission on Achieving Necessary Skills)

The Excellent English Workbook with Audio CD is an essential companion to the Student Book. Each workbook unit provides 14 pages of supplementary practice for its corresponding Student Book unit. The Workbook provides students with further practice with the grammar, vocabulary, listening, reading, writing, and life-skill competencies taught in the Student Book. It offers application lessons that cover competencies in addition to those that are covered in the Student Book.

Features

- **Family Connection** and **Community Connection** lessons provide practice with additional competencies related to the topic of each Student Book unit.

- **Career Connection** lessons build off the Career Connection photo story in the Student Book and address additional work-related competencies.

- **Technology Connection** lessons introduce students to technology objectives as they are used in everyday life, such as using an ATM, email, or a computer calendar.

- **Culture and Communication** activities introduce culturally appropriate communication strategies, such as asking for clarification or repetition.

- **Real-Life Lessons** take learning beyond the classroom as students use new language skills to gather information about their own community through interviews and research.

- **Practice tests** in every unit, complete with CASAS-type listening tasks from the Workbook CD, encourage students to test their skills in a low-stakes environment.

- An **Audio CD**—packaged with each Workbook—includes recorded passages for the Listening and Conversation and Culture and Communication lessons, as well as for the practice tests.

Contents

Unit 4

FINDING A JOB

Unit 5

AILMENTS AND INJURIES

Unit 6

SUCCESS AT WORK

Unit 7

PLACES IN MY LIFE

Unit 8

FOOD AND NUTRITION

Unit 9

AT HOME IN A NEW NEIGHBORHOOD

Unit 10

GETTING AROUND

Unit 11

TALKING ABOUT PLANS

Unit 12

PERSONAL AND EDUCATIONAL GOALS

Correlation Charts

Unit 1 FAMILY AND EDUCATION

LCPs	EE Book 2	LAUSD	EE Book 2	CASAS	EE Book 2
3.15.11 Write legibly upper and lower case letters and demonstrate use of capitalization.	SB: 18, 19 WB: 2, 3, 5	4. Provide basic information about family members. (e.g., *My mom works at a market.*)	SB: 6, 7, 10, 11 WB: 1, 2, 7, 8	0.2.2 Complete a personal information form	SB: 16, 17 WB: 2, 7, 8
3.16.09 Use contractions.	SB: 6, 7 WB: 4, 5	3. Describe physical characteristics (height, weight, hair color, clothing, etc.).	SB: 10, 11 WB: 2, 3, 4	2.6.4 Interpret and order from restaurant and fast food menus, and compute related costs	SB: 6, 7 WB: N/A
3.05.01 Demonstrate ability to report personal information about self or others including a physical description.	SB: 8, 9, 10, 11, 16, 17, 18 WB: 1, 2, 3, 4, 5	2. Use present continuous / progressive tense with events that are a. taking place at the moment (e.g., *She's taking a shower now.*) b. in the immediate future (e.g., *She's going to the doctor this afternoon. He's going shopping this weekend.*)	SB: 18, 19 WB: N/A	7.2.1 Identify and paraphrase pertinent information	SB: 8, 9 WB: 1, 2, 3, 5, 6
3.15.02 Listen to short conversations and answer questions orally and in writing.	SB: 8, 9 WB: 3, 4, 5	20. Use adjectives properly. a. **verb** + **adjective** (e.g., *She looks happy.*) b. **adjective** + **noun** (e.g., *He has a difficult job.*)	SB: 8, 9 WB: 3, 13	0.1.6 Clarify or request clarification	SB: 8, 9, 20 WB: 1, 3, 4, 5
3.08.01 Identify and use ordinal and cardinal numbers.	SB: 10, 11, 14, 15 WB: 1, 2, 3, 5, 6	2. Use ordinal numbers with dates, birth dates, and addresses. (e.g., *She's coming on May. My birthday is December 18.*)	SB: 10, 11, 14, 15 WB: 1, 2, 3, 5, 6	0.1.2 Identify or use appropriate language for informational purposes (e.g., to identify, describe, ask for information, state needs, command, agree or disagree, ask permission)	SB: 6, 7, 10, 11, 16, 17 WB: 2, 3, 4, 5, 6
3.16.07 Use information questions.	SB: 12, 13, 16, 17 WB: 3, 4, 7, 8	3. Use **be** + **going to** to express an intended or planned action (e.g., *I'm going to go to work tomorrow.*)	SB: 8, 9 WB: N/A		
3.16.02 Use common verbs (affirmative, negative, *yes / no* questions, short answers, "wh" questions): – to *be* – simple present tense – simple past-future *will*, "going to" – modals (present) -present continuous	SB: 6, 7, 8, 9, 12, 14, 16, 20 WB: 2, 3, 4, 5	28. Use the following question types: a. Yes / no questions and answers c. Wh- questions and answers with *Who, What, Where, When, Which, Whose, Why,* and *How* (e.g., *How much sugar would you like? How often do you go to the dentist?*)	SB: 12, 13, 14, 15, 16, 17, 20 WB: 4, 5, 8		
3.15.01 Recognize, state, read, and write statements and questions.	SB: 8, 9, 10, 11, 16, 18, 19 WB: 1, 2, 4, 7, 8	6. Interpret and fill out simple personal information forms	SB: 16, 17 WB: 1, 7, 8	0.2.1 Respond appropriately to common personal information questions	SB: 6, 7, 10, 11, 14, 15, 16, 17 WB: 2, 3, 4, 7
3.15.03 Preview and make predictions prior to reading.	SB: 18, 19 WB: 7, 8				
3.15.04 Demonstrate ability to read and comprehend silently and aloud and answer questions	SB: 18, 19 WB: 2, 3, 4	5. Ask and answer personal information questions.	SB: 6, 7, 16, 17 WB: 3, 4, 7, 8		
3.14.01 Identify family relationships.	SB: 6, 7, 10, 11 WB: 1, 2, 3	27. Compute the cost of several items and interpret the bill or receipt. (e.g., *The total comes to $6.95 plus tax.*)	SB: 6, 7 WB: N/A		

Unit 2 IN THE COMMUNITY

LCPs	EE Book 2	LAUSD	EE Book 2	CASAS	EE Book 2
3.16.02 Use common verbs (affirmative, negative, *yes/no* questions, short answers, *"wh"* questions): –*to be* –simple present tense –simple past –future *will*, *"going to"* –modals (present) –present continuous	SB: 22, 23, 24, 25 WB: 1, 2, 3, 4, 5, 6, 7, 8, 9, 10, 11, 12, 13	2. Use present continuous/ progressive tense with events that are a. taking place at the moment (e.g., *She's taking a shower now.*) b. in the immediate future (e.g., *She's going to the doctor this afternoon. He's going shopping this weekend.*)	SB: 22, 23 WB: 1, 2, 3	0.1.2 Identify or use appropriate language for informational purposes (e.g., to identify, describe, ask for information, state needs, command, agree or disagree, ask permission)	SB: 28, 29, 34, 35 WB: pp.3, 4, 5, 6
3.16.07 Use information questions.	SB: 24, 25 WB: 2, 4, 5, 6, 8, 12	9. Use *can* to express ability or inability (e.g., *I can/can't lift it.*)	SB: 28, 29 WB: 4, 5, 6	0.1.3 Identify or use appropriate language to influence or persuade (e.g., to caution, request, advise, persuade, negotiate)	SB: 28, 29, 30, 31 WB: N/A
3.15.01 Recognize, state, read, and write statements and questions.	SB: 26, 27, 28, 29, 30, 34, 36 WB: 4, 5, 6, 8, 12	27. Compute the cost of several items and interpret the bill or receipt. (e.g., *The total comes to $6.95 plus tax.*)	SB: 32, 33 WB: 5	1.3.3 Identify or use various methods to purchase goods and services, and make returns and exchanges	SB: 30, 31 WB: 5, 6
3.15.02 Listen to short conversations and answer questions orally and in writing.	SB: 26, 27 WB: 3, 4, 5	12. Use *may, would, can* and *could* to make formal and informal requests and offers. (e.g., *Would you open the door, please?*)	SB: 28, 29, 30, 32, 32, 33 WB: 3, 4, 5, 6	0.1.6 Clarify or request clarification	SB: 22, 23, 24, 25, 26, 27 WB: 3, 4, 5, 7
		8. Initiate and respond appropriately to simple requests. a. Make polite requests. (e.g., *Could you close the door, please?*) b. Ask for permission. (e.g., *Can/May I leave early?*)	SB: 28, 29, 30, 31 WB: 3, 4, 5, 6		
3.15.03 Preview and make predictions prior to reading.	SB: 30, 31, 34, 35 WB: 7, 8, 9	13. Use *can* and *may* to give or ask permission (e.g., *You may/can leave at any time.*)	SB: 28, 29 WB: 3, 4, 5	1.6.3 Identify procedures the consumer can follow if merchandise or service is unsatisfactory	SB: 30, 31 WB: 1, 2, 3, 4, 5, 6, 7, 8, 9, 10, 11, 12, 13
3.08.01 Identify and use ordinal and cardinal numbers.	SB: 24, 25, 32, 33 WB: 7, 9, 10, 11	33. Describe problems with purchases and communicate the need to return or exchange items. (e.g., *These pants are too small. I'd like a refund please.*)	SB: 30, 31 WB: 6	2.6.4 Interpret and order from restaurant and fast food menus, and compute related costs	SB: 32, 33 WB: N/A
3.15.11 Write legibly upper and lower case letters and demonstrate use of capitalization.	SB: 34, 35 WB: 5, 6	28. Use the following question types: a. *Yes/no* questions and answers c. *Wh*- questions and answers with *Who, What, Where, When, Which, Whose, Why,* and *How* (e.g., *How much sugar would you like? How often do you go to the dentist?*)	SB: 24, 25, 32, 33 WB: 2, 4, 5, 6, 8, 12	0.2.4 Converse about daily and leisure activities and personal interests	SB: 34, 35 WB: 3, 4
3.15.12 Write a basic friendly letter and address an envelope including the return address.	SB: 34, 35 WB: N/A	7. Engage in basic small talk about: a. common activities related to home, school or work. (e.g., *What time is the break?*)	SB: 34, 35 WB: 5		

Unit 3 DAILY ACTIVITIES AT HOME AND SCHOOL

LCPs	EE Book 2	LAUSD	EE Book 2	CASAS	EE Book 2
3.16.02 Use common verbs (affirmative, negative, yes/no questions, short answers, "wh" questions): -to be -simple present tense -simple past -future will, "going to" -modals (present) -present continuous	SB: 38, 39 WB: 1, 2, 3, 4, 5, 6, 7, 8, 9, 10, 11, 12, 13, 14	1. Use of the <u>simple present tense</u> a. the verb *be* in communication about personal information, occupations, feelings, location, names and in descriptions. b. the verbs *want, need, like & hate + infinitive* to express personal wants, needs, likes, and dislikes. c. common verbs used for regularly occurring events.	SB: 38, 39, 40, 41 WB: 1, 2, 3, 4, 5, 6, 7, 8, 9, 10, 11, 12, 13, 14	2.6.1 Interpret information about recreational and entertainment facilities and activities	SB: 46, 47, 48, 49 WB: 4, 5
3.15.11 Write legibly upper and lower case letters and demonstrate use of capitalization.	SB: 48, 49 WB: 2, 3, 4, 5, 8, 11, 12			7.2.1 Identify and paraphrase pertinent information	SB: 44, 45 WB: 3
3.05.01 Demonstrate ability to report personal information about self or others including a physical description.	SB: 52 WB: N/A	4. Use *will* + **verb** to express a future action, a promise.	SB: 38, 39 WB: N/A	7.4.1 Identify or utilize effective study strategies	SB: 48, 49, 52 WB: 6, 13, 14
3.15.07 Demonstrate sequential ordering of events.	SB: 38, 39 WB: 2, 6, 11	59. Order information. a. Put events in chronological order. b. Describe the steps in a process.	SB: 38, 39 WB: 6, 11, 12	2.5.5 Locate and use educational services in the community, including interpreting and writing school-related communications	SB: 48, 49, 50, 51 WB: 4, 6
3.15.05 Read a paragraph.	SB: 50, 51 WB: 1	5. Ask and answer personal information questions.	SB: 40, 41, 48, 49, 52 WB: 10, 13		
3.08.03 Demonstrate use of a calendar by identifying days of the week and months of the year along with the ability to write date in numerical form.	SB: 40, 41 WB: 2, 11	25. Use days in a month to talk about scheduled events.	SB: 42, 43, 46, 47 WB: 2, 3, 11	2.3.2 Identify the months of the year and the days of the week	SB: 42, 43, 46, 47 WB: 2, 3, 11
3.15.09 Write a dictation based on life-skill topics.	SB: 40, 41, 48, 49 WB: 1, 2, 3, 4	29. Use *do/does/did* in questions in the simple present and simple past.	SB: 42, 43 WB: 2, 3, 7	0.1.6 Clarify or request clarification	SB: 38, 39, 48, 49 WB: 3
3.16.08 Use adverbs of time (yesterday, today, and tomorrow) and adverbs of frequency (always, sometimes, and never).	SB: 40, 41 WB: 5, 6	23. Use adverbs of frequency.	SB: 44, 45 WB: 5, 6	2.6.2 Locate information in TV, movie, and other recreational listings	SB: 46, 47, 48, 49 WB: N/A
3.16.07 Use information questions.	SB: 42, 43 WB: 13, 14	22. Interpret simple schedules.	SB: 46, 47, 48, 49 WB: 2, 3, 7, 8, 10, 11		
3.17.01 Demonstrate ability to recognize and pronounce various beginning, middle, and ending sounds.	SB: 42, 43 WB: 3	11. Use clarification strategies.	SB: 48, 49 WB: N/A	0.2.1 Respond appropriately to common personal information questions	SB: 40, 41, 48, 49, 52 WB: 2, 5, 6
3.15.02 Listen to short conversations and answer questions orally and in writing.	SB: 42, 43, 48, 49 WB: 3, 4, 7, 13	13. Identify the structure of the American educational system.	SB: 48, 49 WB: 6, 7, 13		
3.08.01 Identify and use ordinal and cardinal numbers.	SB: 46, 47 WB: 6, 10, 11	26. Use *go* + **verb** + *ing* for communication about leisure activities.	SB: 46, 47 WB: 2, 6, 7	0.1.2 Identify or use appropriate language for informational purposes.	SB: 40, 41, 48, 49, 50, 51, 52 WB: 1, 2, 3, 4, 5, 6, 7, 8, 9, 10, 11, 12, 13, 14
3.15.08 Demonstrate ability to read a simple table or chart.	SB: 46, 47, 48, 49 WB: 6, 7, 8, 10, 11	14. Ask and answer questions about class schedules, school and classroom locations and registration procedures.	SB: 50, 51 WB: 2, 3, 7, 8, 10, 11		
3.15.13 Demonstrate ability to use basic test-taking strategies (circle, bubble in, and dictation).	SB: 46, 47, 50, 51 WB: 13, 14	62. Scan for specific information contained in forms and charts. a. Find words or phrases without reading the whole chart or form. b. Identify key words in comprehension questions about a form or chart.	SB: 48, 49, 52 WB: 2, 6, 7, 8, 10, 11		
3.15.10 Use a bilingual and/or picture dictionary.	SB: 38, 39 WB: 6				
3.15.06 Determine the main idea in a simple paragraph.	SB: 50, 51 WB: 1, 2, 4, 9				

Unit 4 FINDING A JOB

LCPs	EE Book 2	LAUSD	EE Book 2	CASAS	EE Book 2
3.02.02 Demonstrate understanding of basic work-related vocabulary, following instructions, and asking for clarification on the job.	SB: 54, 55, 56, 57 WB: 1, 2, 3, 6	1. Use of the simple present tense with a. the verb *be* in communication about personal information, occupations. b. the verbs *want, need, like & hate + infinitive* to express personal wants, needs, likes, and dislikes	SB: 54, 55, 56, 57, 60, 61 WB: 3, 4	4.4.2 Identify appropriate skills and education for keeping a job	SB: 54, 55 WB: N/A
3.15.08 Demonstrate ability to read a simple table or chart.	SB: 62, 63 WB: 5, 6, 8			4.1.6 Interpret general work-related vocabulary (e.g., experience, swing shift)	SB: 56, 57, 58, 59, 68 WB: 1, 2, 3, 6
3.02.01 Demonstrate understanding of employment expectations, rules, regulations, and safety procedures, including filling our accident reports.	SB: 60, 61, 66, 67 WB: 1	5. Use the simple past tense with a. the verb *be* in communication about past locations. b. common regular verbs to express completed events	SB: 54, 55 WB: 3, 4	4.6.1 Follow, clarify, give, or provide feedback to instructions; give and respond appropriately to criticism	SB: 54, 55 WB: N/A
				4.1.3 Identify and use sources of information about job opportunities	SB: 64, 65 WB: 3, 5, 11
3.01.02 Describe personal work experience and skills.	SB: 54, 55, 68 WB: 4	5. Ask and answer personal information questions.	SB: 58, 59 WB: 4, 9, 11	0.2.1 Respond appropriately to common personal information questions	SB: 56, 57, 58, 59, 68 WB: 4, 9, 11
3.15.01 Recognize, state, read, and write statements and questions.	SB: 56, 57 WB: 2, 3, 4, 9	53. Demonstrate appropriate nonverbal job interview behavior	SB: 68 WB: 4	4.1.5 Identify procedures involved in interviewing for a job, such as arranging for an interview, and acting and dressing appropriately.	SB: 56, 57, 58, 59, 68 WB: 3, 4
3.15.11 Write legibly upper and lower case letters and demonstrate use of capitalization.	SB: 56, 57 WB: 2, 3, 4, 5, 8, 9, 10	29. Use *do/does/did* in questions in the simple present and simple past .	SB: 58, 59 WB: 1, 2, 5	4.1.7 Identify appropriate behavior and attitudes for getting a job	SB: 56, 57, 58, 59, 68 WB: 3, 4
3.15.10 Use a bilingual and/or picture dictionary.	SB: 54, 55 WB: N/A	52. Fill out a simple job application form.	SB: 62, 63, 66, 67 WB: 9, 10, 13, 14	0.1.2 Identify or use appropriate language for informational purposes	SB: 58, 59 WB: 2, 3, 4, 5, 6, 8
3.01.01 Identify different kinds of jobs using simple help-wanted ads including interpreting common abbreviations.	SB: 58, 59, 62, 63 WB: 1, 5, 10, 12	51. Interpret help wanted ads and job announcements, including common abbreviations (e.g., *pt, ft, eves, mo, hr*).	SB: 64, 65 WB: 5, 10, 12	4.8.1 Demonstrate ability to work cooperatively with others as a member of a team.	SB: 60, 61 WB: 10
3.01.06 Demonstrate ability to respond to basic interview questions and recognize acceptable standards of behavior during a job interview.	SB: 68 WB: 3, 4	28. Use the following question types: a. *Yes/no* questions and answers b. *Wh-* questions and answers	SB: 54, 55, 60, 61 WB: 13, 14	4.8.2 Identify ways to learn from others and to help others learn job-related concepts and skills	SB: 60, 61 WB: 8, 11
3.08.01 Identify and use ordinal and cardinal numbers.	SB: 62, 63 WB: 5, 6, 9, 13			7.4.1 Identify or utilize effective study strategies	SB: 64, 65 WB: 13, 14
3.01.03 Demonstrate the ability to fill out a job application, write a resume, and include letters of reference.	SB: 66, 67 WB: 9, 10, 13, 14	62. Scan for specific information contained in forms and charts.	SB: 64, 65 WB: 7, 9, 14	4.2.1 Interpret wages, wage deductions, benefits, and timekeeping forms	SB: 62, 63 WB: 5, 6
3.15.03 Preview and make predictions prior to reading.	SB: 58, 59 WB: 5, 11				
3.02.03 Demonstrate appropriate treatment of co-workers (politeness and respect).	SB: 60, 61 WB: N/A	56. Interpret a simple paycheck stub.	SB: 62, 63 WB: 5, 6	4.1.2 Follow procedures for applying for a job, including interpreting and completing job applications, résumés, and letters of application	SB: 62, 63, 66, 67 WB: 3, 4, 5, 9, 11, 12
3.02.04 Identify parts of a pay stub: wage information, regular, part-time, overtime, deductions, benefits, and taxes.	SB: 60, 61, 62, 63 WB: 5, 6	54. Respond appropriately to job interview questions.	SB: 56, 57, 58, 59, 68 WB: 4	0.2.2 Complete a personal information form	SB: 62, 63, 66, 67 WB: 7, 8, 12

Unit 5 AILMENTS AND INJURIES

LCPs	EE Book 2	LAUSD	EE Book 2	CASAS	EE Book 2
3.07.01 Identify body parts.	SB: 70, 71 WB: 1, 2, 3	45. Interpret simple medical history forms. a. Identify common symptoms. b. Identify common diseases or conditions.	SB: 70, 71, 76, 77, 78, 79 WB: 6, 7, 8, 12	3.1.1 Describe symptoms of illness, including identifying parts of the body; interpret doctor's directions	SB: 70, 71, 74, 75 WB: 1, 2, 4, 7
3.07.02 Define health care vocabulary (emergency room, doctor, nurse, dentist, hospital, clinic, health department, and accident reports).	SB: 70, 71, 72, 73 WB: 1, 2, 3, 4, 5, 6, 7	5. Use the simple past tense with b. common regular verbs to express completed events or actions. c. common irregular verbs to express completed events or actions.	SB: 70, 71, 72, 73, 76, 77 WB: 1, 2, 5, 8, 13, 14	3.1.2 Identify information necessary to make or keep medical and dental appointments	SB: 70, 71, 74, 75, 76, 77 WB: 3
3.15.13 Demonstrate ability to use basic test-taking strategies (circle, bubble in, and dictation).	SB: 74, 75 WB: 13, 14	45. Interpret simple medical history forms. a. Identify common symptoms. b. Identify common diseases or conditions.	SB: 70, 71, 76, 77, 78, 79 WB: 6, 7, 8, 12	3.2.1 Fill out medical health history forms	SB: 70, 71, 76, 77, 78, 79 WB: 12
3.17.01 Demonstrate ability to recognize and pronounce various beginning, middle, and ending sounds.	SB: 74, 75 WB: 3	43. Identify parts of the face and body (eyebrows, lips, ankle, wrist).	SB: 70, 71, 74, 75 WB: 1, 2, 4, 7	2.5.3 Locate medical and health facilities in the community (see also 3.1.3)	SB: 72, 73 WB: N/A
3.07.03 Request doctor's appointment, communicate symptoms and injuries, and follow doctor's instructions.	SB: 70, 71, 74, 75, 78, 79 WB: 3	57. Interpret an employee accident report.	SB: 84 WB: N/A	3.1.3 Identify and utilize appropriate health care services and facilities, including interacting with providers (see also 2.5.3)	SB: 72, 73 WB: 3
3.07.04 Read and interpret information on medicine labels.	SB: 78, 79 WB: 6, 9, 10	46. Identify common prescription and non-prescription medications.	SB: 78, 79 WB: 9, 10	3.3.1 Identify and use necessary medications (see also 3.3.2, 3.3.3)	SB: 78, 79 WB: 9, 10
3.06.01 Demonstrate ability to request operator assistance and use of 911.	SB: 80, 81 WB: N/A	50. Identify procedures for simple first aid and items in first aid kit.	SB: 80, 81, 84 WB: N/A	3.3.3 Identify the difference between prescription, over-the-counter, and generic medications (see also 3.3.1)	SB: 78, 79 WB: N/A
3.15.05 Read a paragraph.	SB: 82, 83 WB: 14	59. Order information. a. Put events in chronological order. b. Describe the steps in a process.	SB: 80, 81, 82, 83 WB: 6, 11, 13, 14	3.3.2 Interpret medicine labels (see also 3.3.1, 3.4.1)	SB: 78, 79 WB: 9, 10
3.02.01 Demonstrate understanding of employment expectations, rules, regulations, and safety procedures, including filling our accident reports.	SB: 84 WB: N/A	44. Make an appointment to see a doctor or dentist.	SB: 70, 71, 74, 75, 76, 77 WB: 3	3.4.3 Interpret procedures for simple first-aid	SB: 80, 81, 84 WB: N/A
3.10.02 Read product label directions, warning signs, and symbols.	SB: 80, 81 WB: 6, 9, 10	47. Interpret simple medicine labels, including dosages. (e.g., *Take two tablets 3 times per day*.)	SB: 78, 79 WB: 6, 9, 10	4.3.4 Report unsafe working conditions and work-related accidents, injuries, and damages	SB: 84 WB: N/A
3.15.07 Demonstrate sequential ordering of events.	SB: 82, 83 WB: 6, 11, 13, 14				
3.10.01 Demonstrate knowledge of emergency procedures at home and work.	SB: 80, 81, 84 WB: N/A				

Unit 6 SUCCESS AT WORK

LCPs	EE Book 2	LAUSD	EE Book 2	CASAS	EE Book 2
3.15.10 Use a bilingual and/or picture dictionary.	SB: 86, 87, 92, 93 WB: 11, 12	5. Use the simple past tense with a. the verb *be* in communication about past locations, feelings, occupations, time references, weather, and personal information. c. common irregular verbs to express completed events or actions (e.g., *ate lunch, went home, did homework*.)	SB: 86, 87, 88, 89 WB: 1, 3, 4, 5, 6, 8, 9, 10, 11, 12, 13, 14	4.4.3 Interpret job-related signs, charts, diagrams, forms, and procedures, and record information on forms, charts, checklists, etc. (See also 4.2.1, 4.3.1, and 4.3.4)	SB: 96, 97 WB: 6, 7
3.02.02 Demonstrate understanding of basic work-related vocabulary, following instructions, and asking for clarification on the job.	SB: 88, 89 WB: 1, 2, 3, 4, 5, 6, 7, 8, 9, 10, 11, 12	52. Fill out a simple job application form. a. Identify basic vocabulary.	SB: 92, 93 WB: 1, 2, 3, 4, 5, 6, 7, 8, 9, 10, 11, 12	4.6.1 Follow, clarify, give, or provide feedback to instructions; give and respond appropriately to criticism	SB: 88, 89 WB: 7, 8, 10, 12
3.15.08 Demonstrate ability to read a simple table or chart.	SB: 90, 91 WB: 2, 8, 12	59. Order information. b. Describe the steps in a process.	SB: 90, 91 WB: 2, 3	7.4.8 Interpret visual representations, such as symbols, blueprints, flowcharts, and schematics (see also 6.6.5)	SB: 90, 91 WB: 2, 11
3.16.02 Use common verbs (affirmative, negative, yes/no questions, short answers, "wh" questions): –to be –simple present tense –simple past –future will, "going to" –modals (present) –present continuous	SB: 92, 93 WB: 1, 3, 4, 5, 6, 10	28. Use the following question types: a. Yes/no questions and answers c. Wh- questions and answers with *Who, What, Where, When, Which, Whose, Why,* and *How* (e.g., *How much sugar would you like? How often do you go to the dentist?*)	SB: 86, 87, 88, 89, 92, 93, 94, 95 WB: 1, 3, 4, 5, 6, 7, 8, 10	0.2.2 Complete a personal information form	SB: 92, 93 WB: 8
				4.6.5 Select and analyze work-related information for a given purpose and communicate it to others orally or in writing	SB: 96, 97 WB: 6, 7
3.01.06 Demonstrate ability to respond to basic interview questions and recognize acceptable standards of behavior during a job interview.	SB: 94, 95, 98, 99, 100 WB: 4, 5, 6, 9	54. Respond appropriately to job interview questions. a. Respond to personal information questions. b. State skills. (e.g., *I can use a cash register.*) c. Answer questions about work history.	SB: 94, 95, 98, 99, 100 WB: 4, 5, 6, 9	4.1.5 Identify procedures involved in interviewing for a job, such as arranging for an interview, acting and dressing appropriately, and selecting appropriate questions and responses	SB: 94, 95, 98, 99, 100 WB: 4, 5, 6, 9
3.01.01 Identify different kinds of jobs using simple help-wanted ads including interpreting common abbreviations.	SB: 96, 97, 98, 99 WB: 2, 7	55. Demonstrate understanding of employee responsibilities. b. Describe a work schedule. (e.g., *I have Mondays off.*)	SB: 96, 97 WB: 6	4.1.3 Identify and use sources of information about job opportunities such as job descriptions, job ads, and announcements, and about the workforce and job market	SB: 96, 97 WB: 7
3.15.12 Write a basic friendly letter and address an envelope including the return address.	SB: 98, 99 WB: 11, 12, 14	29. Use *do/does/did* in questions in the simple present and simple past.	SB: 86, 87, 88, 89, 90, 91 WB: 1, 4, 8	0.2.1 Respond appropriately to common personal information questions	SB: 94, 95, 98, 99, 100 WB: 1, 3, 4, 6
3.01.02 Describe personal work experience and skills.	SB: 100 WB: 4, 5, 6, 9	53. Demonstrate appropriate nonverbal job interview behavior (firm handshake, proper attire, eye contact, etc.).	SB: 94, 95, 98, 99 WB: 4, 5	4.1.2 Follow procedures for applying for a job, including interpreting and completing job applications, résumés, and letters of application	SB: 92, 93 WB: 8
3.16.01 Use subject and object pronouns.	SB: 86, 87, 90, 91 WB: 1, 5 But also addressed in Unit (7)	51. Interpret help wanted ads and job announcements, including common abbreviations (e.g., *pt, ft, eves, mo, hr*).	SB: 96, 97 WB: 7	4.1.6 Interpret general work-related vocabulary (e.g., experience, swing shift)	SB: 94,95, 98, 99, 100 WB: 1, 2, 3, 4, 5, 6, 7, 8, 9, 10, 11, 12
3.16.07 Use information questions.	SB: 96, 97 WB: 1, 3, 4			4.1.7 Identify appropriate behavior and attitudes for getting a job	SB: 94,95, 98, 99, 100 WB: 1, 3, 4, 5, 6, 9

Unit 7 PLACES IN MY LIFE

LCPs	EE Book 2	LAUSD	EE Book 2	CASAS	EE Book 2
3.08.03 Demonstrate use of a calendar by identifying days of the week and months of the year along with the ability to write date in numerical form.	SB: 104, 105 WB: 9, 10	6. Use the past continuous/ progressive tense for communication about events which were happening a. at a definite time in the past (e.g., *I was sleeping at 10:00 last night.*) b. simultaneously with another event (e.g., *I was working while you were sleeping.*)	SB: 102, 103, 104, 105 WB: 1, 3	0.1.2 Identify or use appropriate language for informational purposes (e.g., to identify, describe, ask for information, state needs, command, agree or disagree, ask permission)	SB: 112, 113 WB: 1, 3, 4, 11, 13
3.15.10 Use a bilingual and/or picture dictionary.	SB: 102, 103 WB: 2	38. Inquire about apartment and house rentals. d. Identify proximity to schools, public transportation, shopping, etc.	SB: 112, 113 WB: 11, 12	1.4.2 Select appropriate housing by interpreting classified ads, signs, and other information	SB: 112, 113 WB: 11, 12
3.13.01 Describe various weather conditions and respond appropriately to weather emergencies.	SB: 104, 105 WB: 2, 4, 7, 8, 9, 10	28. Use the following question types: c. Wh- questions and answers with *Who, What, Where, When, Which, Whose, Why,* and *How* (e.g., *How much sugar would you like? How often do you go to the dentist?*)	SB: 104, 105, 106, 107 WB: 1, 3, 4, 11, 13	2.3.2 Identify the months of the year and the days of the week	SB: 104, 105 WB: 9, 10
3.17.01 Demonstrate ability to recognize and pronounce various beginning, middle, and ending sounds.	SB: 106, 107 WB: N/A	20. Use adjectives properly. c. comparative forms with *than* (e.g., *smaller than, more beautiful than, better than, worse than*) d. superlative forms (e.g., *the smallest, the most beautiful, the best, the worst*)	SB: 108, 109, 110, 111, 112, 113, 114, 115 WB: 5, 6, 10, 11	2.3.3 Interpret information about weather conditions	SB: 104, 105 WB: 2, 4, 7, 8, 9, 10
3.17.02 Articulate the sounds associated with consonants.	SB: 106, 107 WB: N/A			7.2.1 Identify and paraphrase pertinent information	SB: 106, 107, 114, 115, 116 WB: 4, 5, 10
3.17.03 Articulate the sounds associated with vowels.	SB: 106, 107 WB: N/A			7.4.2 Take notes or write a summary or an outline	SB: 106, 107, 116 WB: 5, 6, 7, 9, 10
3.08.01 Identify and use ordinal and cardinal numbers. 3.12.01 Identify places in the community and describe public services.	SB: 112, 113 WB: 6, 7, 9, 11, 12			7.4.5 Use reference materials, such as dictionaries and encyclopedias	SB: 102, 103 WB: N/A
3.15.05 Read a paragraph.	SB: 112, 113 WB: 1, 2				
3.15.02 Listen to short conversations and answer questions orally and in writing.	SB: 106, 107, 116 WB: 3, 4, 8				
3.15.09 Write a dictation based on life-skill topics.	SB: 106, 107 WB: 2, 3, 4, 5, 6				

Unit 8 FOOD AND NUTRITION

LCPs	EE Book 2	LAUSD	EE Book 2	CASAS	EE Book 2
3.11.01 Identify food items and interpret food packaging and labels.	SB: 120, 121, 122, 123, 128, 129 WB: 1, 2, 5, 6, 9	16. Use nouns appropriately. e. partitives (e.g., *a bunch of bananas, a jar of peanut butter*)	SB: 120, 121, 126, 127 WB: 1, 2, 3	1.6.1 Interpret food packaging labels (see also 1.2.1, 3.5.1)	SB: 120, 121, 122, 123, 126, 127, 128, 129, 130, 131 WB: 5, 6, 9
3.15.10 Use a bilingual and/or picture dictionary.	SB: 120, 121, 126, 127 WB: 1	35. Interpret basic information on food packaging and labels.	SB: 122, 123, 128, 129 WB: 5, 6, 9	7.4.5 Use reference materials, such as dictionaries and encyclopedias	SB: 120, 121, 126, 127 WB: 1
3.15.13 Demonstrate ability to use basic test-taking strategies (circle, bubble in, and dictation).	SB: 122, 123 WB: 13, 14	34. Identify and ask for typical containers and quantities of common foods. (e.g., *I need two large cans of tuna. I'd like a dozen eggs.*)	SB: 122, 123, 124, 125 WB: 2, 3	1.2.1 Interpret advertisements, labels, charts, and price tags in selecting goods and services	SB: 122, 123, 128, 129, 130, 131 WB: 3, 9
3.08.05 Count and use U.S. coins and currency demonstrating the ability to also write the amounts.	SB: 124, 125 WB: 3, 4, 9, 10	9. Initiate and respond appropriately to invitations and offers. a. Invite or offer politely. (e.g., *Would you like to go to the park? Would you like some coffee?*)	SB: 124, 125 WB: 2, 3, 4	3.5.1 Interpret nutritional and related information listed on food labels (see also 1.6.1)	SB: 122, 123, 126, 127, 128, 129, 130, 131 WB: 5, 6, 10, 11, 12
3.07.05 Identify basic foods and food groups, recognize nutritional information on food labels, and understand the order of ingredients.	SB: 122, 123, 126, 127, 128, 129, 130, 131 WB: 1, 5, 6, 11, 12	28. Use the following question types: c. Wh- questions and answers with *Who, What, Where, When, Which, Whose, Why,* and *How* (e.g., *How much sugar would you like? How often do you go to the dentist?*)	SB: 126, 127 WB: 3, 5, 9, 10, 13, 14	0.1.4 Identify or use appropriate language in general social situations (e.g., to greet, introduce, thank, apologize, compliment, express pleasure or regret)	SB: 124, 125 WB: 2, 3, 4
3.15.08 Demonstrate ability to read a simple table or chart.	SB: 128, 129 WB: 2, 3, 11, 12	27. Compute the cost of several items and interpret the bill or receipt. (e.g., *The total comes to $6.95 plus tax.*)	SB: 124, 125 WB: 2, 3, 9, 10	1.3.8 Identify common food items	SB: 122, 123, 124, 125, 134 WB: 1, 2
3.12.03 Interpret restaurant menus, cost of a meal and tips.	SB: 124, 125 WB: 3, 4	17. Use determiners appropriately. e. quantifiers: *any, some, many, much, a lot of, a little, a few, none, another, other, each, every*	SB: 120, 121, 122, 123, 124, 125, 126, 127, 128, 129, 130, 131 WB: 3, 4, 5, 6	2.6.4 Interpret and order from restaurant and fast food menus, and compute related costs	SB: 124, 125 WB: 4, 9, 10
3.15.07 Demonstrate sequential ordering of events.	SB: 132, 133 WB: 2, 6, 7, 8, 12, 13, 14	29. Use *do / does / did* in questions in the simple present and simple past.	SB: 126, 127 WB: 9	3.5.2 Select a balanced diet	SB: 126, 127 WB: 5, 6, 11, 12
		36. Read and order from a simple menu.	SB: 134 WB: 3, 4	3.5.3 Interpret food storage information	SB: 126, 127 WB: N/A
				1.1.1 Interpret recipes	SB: 132, 133 WB: 7, 8
				1.1.7 Identify product containers and interpret weight and volume	SB: 122, 123, 124, 125 WB: 5, 6, 9
				7.2.2 Analyze a situation, statement, or process, identifying component elements and causal and part/whole relationships	SB: 132, 133 WB: 2, 11, 12, 13

Unit 9 AT HOME IN A NEW NEIGHBORHOOD

LCPs	EE Book 2	LAUSD	EE Book 2	CASAS	EE Book 2
3.15.10 Use a bilingual and/or picture dictionary.	SB: 134, 135 WB: 6	20. Use adjectives properly. d. superlative forms (e.g., *the smallest, the most beautiful, the best, the worst*)	SB: 134, 135, 136, 137, 146, 147 WB: 1, 2, 5	1.7.4 Interpret maintenance procedures for household appliances and personal possessions	SB: 146, 147 WB: 10
3.11.04 Identify types of housing (apartment, house, mobile home, condominium) and decipher a lease rental agreement.	SB: 136, 137, 138, 139 WB: 2, 7, 8	23. Ask for and give simple directions to community locations. a. Interpret simple written directions. b. Locate places on a map. (e.g., *It's between Colorado and Broadway.*)	SB: 140, 141 WB: 2	1.4.1 Identify different kinds of housing, areas of the home, and common household items	SB: 136, 137 WB: 2, 9
				1.4.2 Select appropriate housing by interpreting classified ads, signs, and other information	SB: 136, 137, 138, 139, 148 WB: 2, 3
3.11.05 Identify basic utility companies (water, gas, electric, telephone, and cable).	SB: 140, 141, 144, 145 WB: 6, 7, 9, 10	37. Interpret signs and ads for rental units, including abbreviations (*2 bd./1 ba., See mgr.*).	SB: 138, 139 WB: 2, 3, 12	1.4.4 Interpret information to obtain, maintain, or cancel housing utilities	SB: 140, 141, 144, 145 WB: 9, 10
3.17.03 Articulate the sounds associated with vowels.	SB: 142, 143 WB: N/A	27. Use affirmative and negative statements.	SB: 138, 139 WB: 3, 4	1.4.3 Interpret lease and rental agreements	SB: 138, 139 WB: 7, 8
3.06.04 Demonstrate ability to operate public and cellular telephones, pagers, and use a telephone card.	SB: 144, 145 WB: 4, 10	1. Use of the simple present tense with a. the verb *be* in communication about personal information, occupations, feelings, location, names and in descriptions of objects, people, time, and the weather.	SB: 140, 141 WB: 5, 6, 13, 14	1.4.7 Interpret information about home maintenance, and communicate housing problems to a landlord (see also 1.7.4)	SB: 146, 147 WB: 6, 10
		29. Use *do/does/did* in questions in the simple present and simple past.	SB: 140, 141, 142, 143 WB: 5, 8	1.4.5 Interpret information about tenant and landlord rights	SB: 138, 139 WB: 8
		28. Use the following question types: a. *Yes/no* questions and answers c. *Wh-* questions and answers with *Who, What, Where, When, Which, Whose, Why,* and *How* (e.g., *How much sugar would you like? How often do you go to the dentist?*)	SB: 140, 141, 142, 143, 144, 145 WB: 5, 6, 7, 11, 13, 14	2.5.4 Read, interpret, and follow directions found on public signs and building directories (see also 1.3.7)	SB: 140, 141 WB: N/A
		27. Compute the cost of several items and interpret the bill or receipt. (e.g., *The total comes to $6.95 plus tax.*)	SB: 144, 145 WB: 3, 9	2.1.8 Use the telephone to make and receive routine personal and business calls	SB: 144, 145 WB: 3, 4, 7, 13, 14
		39. Describe maintenance and repairs needed in a rental unit. (e.g., *The roof is leaking.*)	SB: 146, 147 WB: 6	2.2.1 Ask for, give, follow, or clarify directions (see also 1.1.3, 1.9.4, 2.2.5)	SB: 140, 141 WB: 3, 4, 6
		38. Inquire about apartment and house rentals. a. Describe features of a unit (furnished, unfurnished).	SB: 138, 139, 148 WB: 3, 4, 11	2.6.4 Interpret and order from restaurant and fast food menus, and compute related costs	SB: 144, 145 WB: This may be better be placed on the Unit with Food.
				7.4.5 Use reference materials, such as dictionaries and encyclopedias	SB: 134, 135 WB: 12

Unit 10 GETTING AROUND

LCPs	EE Book 2	LAUSD	EE Book 2	CASAS	EE Book 2
3.15.10 Use a bilingual and/or picture dictionary.	SB: 150, 151, 156, 157 WB: N/A	11. Use expressions of necessity with a. *have to* (e.g., *I have to learn English to get a good job.*) b. *must* (e.g., *You must have a driver's license to drive.*)	SB: 150, 151, 152, 153 WB: 1, 2, 3	1.9.2 Identify driving regulations and procedures to obtain a driver's license (see also 2.5.7)	SB: 150, 151, 154, 155 WB: 1, 9, 10
3.09.06 Identify safe driving practices (seat belts, child safety restraints).	SB: 152, 153 WB: 13, 14	15. Use *should* to communicate advisability (e.g., *You shouldn't smoke.*)	SB: 152, 153 WB: 4	1.9.8 Interpret information about automobile insurance	SB: 150, 151, 154, 155 WB: 7, 8
3.09.05 Identify required documents related to transportation (driver's license, insurance card, registration, passport).	SB: 150, 151, 154, 155 WB: 1, 9, 10	23. Ask for and give simple directions to community locations. a. Interpret simple written directions. b. Locate places on a map. (e.g., *It's between Colorado and Broadway.*)	SB: 152, 153, 158, 159, 160, 161, 162, 163 WB: 11, 12	2.2.1 Ask for, give, follow, or clarify directions (see also 1.1.3, 1.9.4, 2.2.5)	SB: 152, 153, 156, 157, 158, 159, 160, 161, 162, 163 WB: 11, 12
3.09.03 Demonstrate ability to read a map, locate places, follow simple instructions related to geographical directions (N, S, E, W; right, left).	SB: 158, 159, 160, 161, 162, 163 WB: 11, 12	22. Use prepositions. a. of place (e.g., *over, across, beside*) b. of direction (e.g., *through, toward, into, out of*) c. of time (e.g., *in, on, at, from...to*).	SB: 156, 157, 158, 159 WB: 4, 6, 11, 12	2.5.4 Read, interpret, and follow directions found on public signs and building directories (see also 1.3.7)	SB: 152, 153, 158, 159, 160, 161, 162, 163 WB: 9
3.12.01 Identify places in the community and describe public services.	SB: 158, 159, 160, 161 WB: 9	8. Use inclusive commands (e.g., *Let's move the table.*) and a series of negative or affirmative commands (e.g., *Sit down and roll up your sleeve.*)	SB: 156, 157 WB: 5	2.5.7 Interpret permit and license requirements (see also 1.9.2)	SB: 150, 151, 154, 155 WB: 1, 9, 10
				5.3.6 Interpret information or identify requirements for establishing residency and/or obtaining citizenship	SB: 150, 151, 154, 155 WB: 9, 10
				7.2.1 Identify and paraphrase pertinent information	SB: 156, 157 WB: 13, 14
				7.4.5 Use reference materials, such as dictionaries and encyclopedias	SB: 156, 157 WB: 12

Unit 11 TALKING ABOUT PLANS

LCPs	EE Book 2	LAUSD	EE Book 2	CASAS	EE Book 2
3.15.10 Use a bilingual and/or picture dictionary.	SB: 166, 167, 172, 173 WB: 2, 5, 7	26. Use **go + verb + ing** for communication about leisure activities (e.g., *Do you want to go bowling? I went camping.*)	SB: 166, 167, 168, 169, 170, 171 WB: 1, 2, 3, 4	0.1.2 Identify or use appropriate language for informational purposes (e.g., to identify, describe, ask for information, state needs, command, agree or disagree, ask permission)	SB: 168, 169, 170, 171 WB: 10, 11, 12, 13, 14
3.08.03 Demonstrate use of a calendar by identifying days of the week and months of the year along with the ability to write date in numerical form.	SB: 172, 173, 174, 175, 176, 177 WB: 6, 8	9. Initiate and respond appropriately to invitations and offers. a. Invite or offer politely. (e.g., *Would you like to go to the park? Would you like some coffee?*) b. Refuse politely with an excuse. (e.g., *I'm sorry, I can't go. I have to work.*) c. Accept an invitation or offer. (e.g., *Thanks, I'd love to.*)	SB: 168, 19 WB: 1, 3, 4	0.1.4 Identify or use appropriate language in general social situations (e.g., to greet, introduce, thank, apologize, compliment, express pleasure or regret)	SB: 168, 169 WB: 1, 3, 4, 13, 14
				0.2.1 Respond appropriately to common personal information questions	SB: 170, 171 WB: 1, 3, 4
3.17.01 Demonstrate ability to recognize and pronounce various beginning, middle, and ending sounds.	SB: 170, 171 WB: N/A	3. Use **be + going** to to express an intended or planned action (e.g., *I'm going to go to work tomorrow.*)	SB: 170, 171, 178, 179 WB: 1, 2	2.3.2 Identify the months of the year and the days of the week	SB: 172, 173, 174, 175 WB: 6, 8, 11
3.09.02 Identify transportation costs, schedules and practices (exact change, tips).	SB: 176, 177 WB: 6, 8, 9, 10, 11	4. Use **will + verb** to express a future action, a promise (e.g., *I'll be right back*) or prediction (e.g., *Don't worry. She'll help you.*)	SB: 172, 173 WB: 5, 6	2.6.1 Interpret information about recreational and entertainment facilities and activities	SB: 176, 177 WB: 7, 8
3.12.04 Demonstrate understanding of holidays and social customs.	SB: 172, 173, 174, 175 WB: 1, 2, 3, 4	28. Use the following question types: c. Wh- questions and answers with *Who, What, Where, When, Which, Whose, Why,* and *How* (e.g., *How much sugar would you like? How often do you go to the dentist?*)	SB: 166, 167, 174, 175 WB: 1, 6, 10	2.6.2 Locate information in TV, movie, and other recreational listings	SB: 176, 177 WB: 7, 8
				2.7.1 Interpret information about holidays	SB: 172, 173, 174, 175 WB: 5
3.15.08 Demonstrate ability to read a simple table or chart.	SB: 176, 177 WB: 6, 8, 9, 11	22. Interpret simple schedules (recreation center, health clinic, TV guide).	SB: 176, 177 WB: 7, 8	7.2.1 Identify and paraphrase pertinent information	SB: 178, 179 WB: 3, 10
3.15.01 Recognize, state, read, and write statements and questions.	SB: 178, 179 WB: 1, 2, 3, 4, 5, 6, 9, 10, 11	13. Use can and may to give or ask permission (e.g., *You may/can leave at any time.*)	SB: 172, 173, 178, 179 WB: 7, 8	7.4.2 Take notes or write a summary or an outline	SB: 178, 179 WB: 7, 8, 9
3.15.05 Read a paragraph.	SB: 178, 179 WB: 2, 9, 14	55. Demonstrate understanding of employee responsibilities. a. Call in sick/late.	SB: 180 WB: 11, 12	7.4.5 Use reference materials, such as dictionaries and encyclopedias	SB: 166, 167, 172, 173 WB: 7
		12. Use *may, would, can* and *could* to make formal and informal requests and offers. (e.g., *Would you open the door, please?*)	SB: 172, 173 WB: 5, 6	4.6.5 Select and analyze work-related information for a given purpose and communicate it to others orally or in writing	SB: 180 WB: 11, 12
		7. Engage in basic small talk about: a. common activities related to home, school or work. (e.g., *What time is the break?*)	SB: 168, 169, 170, 171 WB: 3, 4, 10	0.2.4 Converse about daily and leisure activities and personal interests	SB: 168, 169, 170, 171 WB: 1, 3, 4
		5. Ask and answer personal information questions.	SB: 170, 171 WB: 3, 4, 10	0.1.6 Clarify or request clarification	SB: 166, 167 WB: 4

LCPs	EE Book 2	LAUSD	EE Book 2	CASAS	EE Book 2
3.09.05 Identify required documents related to transportation (driver's license, insurance card, registration, passport).	SB: 182, 183 WB: 1, 13, 14	8. Use inclusive commands (e.g., *Let's move the table.*) and a series of negative or affirmative commands (e.g., *Sit down and roll up your sleeve.*)	SB: 182, 183 WB: N/A	7.4.5 Use reference materials, such as dictionaries and encyclopedias	SB: 182, 183, 188, 189 WB: 12
		3. Use **be + going** to to express an intended or planned action (e.g., *I'm going to go to work tomorrow.*)	SB: 182, 183, 188, 189 WB: 3, 4, 5, 11	0.2.2 Complete a personal information form	SB: 192, 193 WB: N/A
		13. Identify the structure of the American educational system (including pre- school, K-12, and post-secondary).	SB: WB: 5	0.2.1 Respond appropriately to common personal information questions	SB: 184, 185 WB: 1, 2, 3
3.15.11 Write legibly upper and lower case letters and demonstrate use of capitalization.	SB: 194, 195 WB: 1, 2, 3, 4	28. Use the following question types: c. *Wh-* questions and answers with *Who, What, Where, When, Which, Whose, Why,* and *How* (e.g., *How much sugar would you like? How often do you go to the dentist?*)	SB: 190, 191 WB: 3, 11, 13, 14		
3.15.10 Use a bilingual and/or picture dictionary.	SB: 182, 183, 188, 189 WB: 2	7. Engage in basic small talk about: a. common activities related to home, school or work. (e.g., *What time is the break?*) b. states of being, the weather. (e.g., *I'm really tired. It's hot today.*)	SB: 186, 187, 192, 193 WB: 3, 4, 5	0.2.4 Converse about daily and leisure activities and personal interests	SB: 186, 187, 192, 193 WB: 3, 4, 5
		1. Use of the simple present tense with a. the verb be in communication about personal information, occupations, feelings, location, names and in descriptions of objects, people, time, and the weather. b. the verbs *want, need, like & hate* + **infinitive** to express personal wants, needs, likes, and dislikes (e.g., *She likes to play soccer.*) c. common verbs used for regularly occurring events. (e.g., *I usually get up at 6:30 a.m.*)	SB: 184, 185, 188, 189 WB: 2, 7, 10	2.5.5 Locate and use educational services in the community, including interpreting and writing school-related communications	SB: 194, 195 WB: N/A
		2. Use present continuous/progressive tense with events that are a. taking place at the moment (e.g., *She's taking a shower now.*) b. in the immediate future (e.g., *She's going to the doctor this afternoon. He's going shopping this weekend.*)	SB: 188, 189 WB: 4, 5, 10	0.1.2 Identify or use appropriate language for informational purposes (e.g., to identify, describe, ask for information, state needs, command, agree or disagree, ask permission)	SB: 184, 185, 186, 187, 192, 193 WB: 1, 2, 3, 4, 5, 6, 7, 8, 9, 10, 11, 12
		4. Use will + **verb** to express a future action, a promise (e.g., *I'll be right back.*) or prediction (e.g., *Don't worry. She'll help you.*)	SB: 188, 189, 190, 191 WB: 5, 6, 10		
		5. Use the simple past tense with a. the verb *be* in communication about past locations, feelings, occupations, time references, weather, and personal information. b. common regular verbs to express completed events or actions (e.g., *worked, played, visited.*) c. common irregular verbs to express completed events or actions (e.g., *ate lunch, went home, did homework.*)	SB: 188, 189 WB: 4, 5		
		27. Compute the cost of several items and interpret the bill or receipt. (e.g., *The total comes to $6.95 plus tax.*)	SB: 190, 191 WB: 7, 8, 9, 10, 12		
		6. Interpret and fill out simple personal information forms (e.g. *school registration forms*).	SB: 192, 193 WB: N/A		
		27. Use affirmative and negative statements.	SB: 182, 183 WB: 1, 3, 4, 11		

Letters and Numbers

1 LISTEN AND CIRCLE. Listen to the letters. Circle the one you hear.

WCD, 2

1. m	(n)	o	
2. s	f	h	
3. b	c	d	

4. a	e	i	
5. b	d	v	
6. u	y	w	

7. e	u	o	
8. r	l	a	
9. z	c	e	

2 LISTEN AND WRITE the missing letters.

WCD, 3

1. _R_ a u _l_

2. B i ____ ____

3. ____ o ____ ____ a

4. O ____ ____ a ____

5. ____ a f ____ ____ l

6. R o ____ e ____ ____ o

3 WRITE the words in the chart.

Canada	Cuba	David	Haiti	Jake	Korea
Lisa	Maria	Mexico	Rob	Sara	Taiwan

First names	Countries

4 WRITE. Complete the conversation. Use the words in the box.

David	Hi	name	Taiwan	Yolanda

A: ____Hi____. I'm David.

B: It's nice to meet you, _____. I'm _____.

A: How do you spell your _____?

B: Y-O-L-A-N-D-A.

A: Where are you from, Yolanda?

B: I'm from Mexico. And you?

A: I'm from _____.

5 WRITE AND TALK. Complete the conversation. Write about you and a partner. Then practice it with your partner.

A: Hi. I'm _____.

B: It's nice to meet you, _____. I'm _____.

A: How do you spell your name?

B: _____.

A: Where are you from, _____?

B: I'm from _____.

6 WRITE. Unscramble the months.

1. a r u J n y a ____January____

2. y e b F u a r r _____

3. c r a h M _____

4. l p A i r _____

5. y a M _____

6. e u J n _____

7. y J l u _____

8. s A g t u u _____

9. r m b t e e S p e _____

10. e r t c b o O _____

11. e e o r m b N v _____

12. e D r m b c e e _____

WCD, 4

7 LISTEN AND CIRCLE the birthday you hear.

1. January 7th   February 7th

2. October 25th   November 25th

3. March 13th   May 13th

4. September 1st   November 1st

5. August 20th   April 20th

6. December 30th   November 30th

7. June 17th   July 17th

8. April 16th   August 16th

8 MATCH the question and the answer.

_____ 1. What is your name?

_____ 2. Where are you from?

_____ 3. How do you spell your name?

_____ 4. May I borrow your pen?

_____ 5. What time is it?

_____ 6. What does absent mean?

_____ 7. Can you repeat that, please?

a. Absent means not here.

b. I said, "Open your book to page 3."

c. Yes, you can borrow my pen.

d. My name is Luis.

e. It's 9 o'clock.

f. I'm from Mexico.

g. L-U-I-S.

Grammar

1 **CIRCLE** the nouns and underline the adjectives.

1. (Marta) is <u>pretty</u>.
2. My apartment is small.
3. Is your teacher nice?
4. New York City is big and noisy.

5. Jake is tall.
6. The school is large.
7. My car is clean.
8. The children are happy.

2 **CIRCLE** the pronouns and underline the adjectives.

1. Marta and Sue are friends. (They) are very <u>nice</u>.
2. The car is old, but it is clean.
3. Here are the children. They are very happy today.
4. The apartment is nice, but it is very loud.
5. This is Portland. It is very beautiful.
6. Here is the school. It is new and very large.

3 **MATCH** the picture and the sentence.

_____d_____

_____

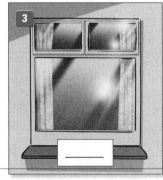
_____

_____

a. He is young.
b. It is clean.
c. They are old.
d. She is happy.

4 **UNSCRAMBLE** the sentences. Then underline the verbs.

1. very nice / teacher / is / My / .
   My teacher is very nice.

2. you / How / are / ?
   _____

3. loud music / likes / Jake / .
   _____

4. absent today / They / are / .
   _____

5. to / school / I / go / at 8:00 A.M. / .
   _____

6. Chinese / speaks / She / .
   _____

Grammar: Parts of Speech

5 **WRITE** the words in the chart.

clean	eat	~~happy~~	I	is	it	old	San Diego
school	she	speak	teacher	they	T.V.	worked	young

Nouns	Pronouns	Adjectives	Verbs
		happy	

6 **MATCH** the punctuation and the name.

 __e__ 1. A, B, C   a. small letters

_____ 2. .   b. exclamation point

_____ 3. ?   c. comma

_____ 4. !   d. period

_____ 5. ,   e. capital letters

_____ 6. a, b, c   f. question mark

7 **LOOK AND CIRCLE** the words in the puzzle.

absent	are	~~birthday~~
clean	comma	happy
old	period	speak
teacher	they	young

Y	O	U	N	G	D	E
A	P	S	D	L	O	E
D	T	P	T	Y	I	P
H	N	E	A	H	R	Y
T	E	A	C	H	E	R
R	S	K	E	K	P	Y
I	B	R	A	L	B	T
B	A	M	M	O	C	N

Lesson 1

1 **MATCH** the words and pictures.

a. divorced   c. single   e. adults

b. engaged   d. twins   f. widowed

2 **WRITE.** Complete the sentences. Use the correct negative or affirmative form of the verb *be*.

1. Jack and Jane _____are_____ engaged. The wedding date is April 4th.

2. I'm not 30 years old. I _____ 35 years old.

3. I'm single. I _____ married.

4. Mr. and Mrs. Lee are married. They _____ single.

5. Sara is married. She _____ divorced.

6. He isn't my cousin. He _____ my brother.

3 **WRITE.** Complete the paragraph. Use the correct negative or affirmative form of the verb *be*.

My name (1) _____is_____ Ana. I (2) _____ married. My husband and I

(3) _____ from Mexico. We have two children and two grandchildren. Roberto

(4) _____ our older son. Roberto (5) _____ divorced. He has two children, Sofia

and Rafael. Sofia and Rafael (6) _____ twins. Tomas (7) _____ our younger son.

Tomas (8) _____ married now, but he is engaged. The wedding date (9) _____

soon! We (10) _____ all very excited!

Lesson 2

1 WRITE. Put the words into the correct places in the chart. Some words can go in more than one place.

beard	blonde	brown	curly	freckles	~~glasses~~	long
mustache	short	straight	tall	~~thin~~	~~wavy~~	green

Words to describe . . .			
Hair	**Eyes**	**Bodies**	**Faces**
wavy		*thin*	*glasses*

2 WRITE. Complete the paragraph about the picture. Use *is, isn't, are, has,* or *have*.

This (1) ____is____ a picture of Mike and Lisa. Mike and Lisa (2) _____ married. They both (3) _____ glasses, but they look very different. Mike (4) _____ tall and thin. He (5) _____ a mustache and a beard. He (6) _____ curly brown hair and brown eyes. Lisa (7) _____ tall. She (8) _____ short. She (9) _____ long brown hair. She also (10) _____ freckles.

3 WRITE. Complete the crossword puzzle.

ACROSS

3. She isn't married. She is _____ .
5. Mr. and Mrs. Garcia are _____ .
6. I see better with _____ .
7. not tall

DOWN

1. a hair color
2. hair on the face
3. not curly
4. Tomas and Suzy are _____ . The wedding date is May 5.

Lesson 3

1 **LISTEN.** Write the numbers under the pictures.

WCD, 5

A ____1____

B _____

C _____

D _____

E _____

F _____

2 **LISTEN** to the question. Then listen to the conversation. Fill in the correct answer.

WCD, 6

1. Ⓐ   Ⓑ   Ⓒ

2. Ⓐ   Ⓑ   Ⓒ

3. Ⓐ   Ⓑ   Ⓒ

3 **WRITE.** Complete the conversation. Use the words in the box.

brown hair and glasses	he	husband	I'm	is	tall and heavy

A: _____*I'm*_____ looking for my _____.

B: What does _____ look like?

A: He's _____. He has _____.

B: There he _____.

A: Oh, thank you!

Culture and Communication—*Describing People*

WCD, 7

1 **LISTEN** and read. Then practice with a partner.

1. *A:* This is my sister. She's fat.

   B: No, she isn't! She's a little overweight.

2. *A:* This is my cousin Lisa. She's tall and skinny.

   B: No, she isn't. She's tall and thin.

3. *A:* This is my dad. He's old.

   B: No, he isn't. He's middle-aged.

4. *A:* This is my grandfather. He's really old!

   B: No, he isn't. He's a senior citizen.

Useful Expressions			
Ways to Describe People			
Not *fat*, but	plump	overweight	heavy
Not *skinny*, but	slender	thin	petite
Not *old*, but	older	middle-aged (40-55)	elderly (65+) (be) a senior citizen (65+)

2 **WRITE** sentences about your family and friends. Use words from the box. You can use negatives.

1. _____

2. _____

3. _____

4. _____

5. _____

6. _____

3 **TALK**. Tell a partner about your family and friends. Use words from the box. You can use negatives.

Lesson 4

1 **MATCH** the answer to the correct question.

___d___ 1. Are you in my class?   a. It's June 15th.

_____ 2. Is he our teacher?   b. Marie.

_____ 3. What is your name?   c. No, he isn't.

_____ 4. When is summer vacation?   d. Yes, I am.

_____ 5. Where is the school?   e. She's my sister.

_____ 6. Who is she?   f. It's on Pine Street.

2 **WRITE.** Unscramble the questions.

1. I / Am / in / your / class / ?
   _Am I in your class?_____

2. she / your / teacher / Is / ?
   _____

3. he / Is / in / high school / ?
   _____

4. the / teacher / is / Who / ?
   _____

5. is / Where / the / school / ?
   _____

6. your / birthday / When / is / ?
   _____

3 **WRITE** a question for each answer.

1. _____? Yes, I am.

2. _____? It's Mrs. Sanchez.

3. _____? It's Pine Street Elementary School.

4. _____? No, I'm not.

5. _____? It's February 11th.

6. _____? It's 411 Pine Street.

Lesson 5

WCD, 8

1 **LISTEN** and circle the number you hear.

1. 30   30th
2. 17   17th
3. 15th   50th
4. 4th   40th
5. 16   60
6. 18th   80th

WCD, 9

2 **LISTEN** and write the number you hear.

1. He's in the _____ grade.
2. We live on _____ Street.
3. Spring vacation is March _____ .
4. My son is _____ years old.
5. Today is my grandmother's _____ birthday.
6. The address is _____ Oak Street.

WCD, 10

3 **LISTEN.** Write the student's name in the correct place in the calendar.

Dani	Katy	Michael	Pedro	Tony	Will

February						
Sunday	**Monday**	**Tuesday**	**Wednesday**	**Thursday**	**Friday**	**Saturday**
1	2	3	4	5	6	7
8	9	10	11	12	13	14
15	16	17	18	19	20	21
22	23	24	25	26	27	28

Family Connection—*Understanding Emergency Forms*

1 **READ** the emergency information form.

Washington Street School – Emergency Information Form

Student name: _Ana Garcia_   Grade/Class: _9th Grade_

Address: _476 Pine Street_   Phone number: _(619) 555-9786_

San Diego, CA 92102

Date of birth: _February 11, 1997_   Do you have health insurance?   (Yes)   No

Who do we call in an emergency?

Name: _Maria Garcia_   Relationship: _Mother_

Home phone: _(619) 555-9786_   Work phone: _(619) 555-6345_

Your doctor: _Dr. Lisa Lee_   Your doctor's phone number: _(619) 555-2378_

2 **CIRCLE** date of birth, grade, an emergency contact name, relationship, and doctor in the form in Activity 1.

3 **MATCH** the words and meanings.

___e___ 1. an emergency   a. a person who takes care of sick people

_____ 2. date of birth   b. birthday

_____ 3. doctor   c. money to pay for health problems

_____ 4. health insurance   d. how people are connected

_____ 5. relationship   e. a bad thing that happens; it's usually a surprise

3 CIRCLE *yes* or *no*.

1. There is a fire.   (yes)   no
2. Salim calls the fire department.   yes   no
3. The emergency is at Salim's house.   yes   no
4. Salim is at his house.   yes   no
5. The police are coming to Salim's house.   yes   no
6. Salim's address is 6106 Oak Street.   yes   no
7. The phone number is 555-9867.   yes   no

4 REAL-LIFE LESSON. Get emergency numbers. Write them in the chart.

Emergency Numbers	
"911"	*911*
Police	
Fire	
Poison Control	
Hospital	
Family / friend (name) _____	
Other _____	

Career Connection — *Using a Phone Directory*

Oscar wants information about benefits. He has a company phone directory. A directory is a list of names and telephone numbers.

1 READ part of a company phone directory.

Grand Restaurants, Inc.		
Department	Contact person	Number
Accounting		
Billing	Sue Scott	555-9840
Payroll	Mark Green	555-9841
Facilities		
Room Reservations	Gary Wong	555-9842
Safety	David Brown	555-9843
Human Resources		
Benefits	Linda Smith	555-9844
Training	Robert Hart	555-9845
Information Technology		
Corporate Systems	Tony Valdez	555-9846
Help Desk	Amy Nguyen	555-9847
Service & Repairs	Nick Roberts	555-9848

2 CIRCLE the correct words.

1. The directory is for a company called **Grand Restaurants** / **Accounting.**

2. 555-9841 is a **phone number** / **department**.

3. Accounting is a **department** / **contact person**.

4. Amy Nguyen is a **contact person** / **department**.

5. There are **four** / **five** departments in this part of the directory.

6. Information about benefits is in the **Facilities** / **Human Resources** department.

7. You call **Robert Hart** / **Linda Smith** for information about benefits.

8. Linda Smith's phone number is **555-9844** / **555-9843**.

3 READ AND CIRCLE. Oscar calls Linda Smith. He wants information about benefits. Read the phone conversation. Circle the correct words.

Linda: Hello. This is **Linda** / **Oscar** Smith.

Oscar: **Hello** / **Goodbye**, Linda. My **name** / **number** is Oscar Santos. I'd like some information about **benefits** / **computers**.

Linda: Sure, Oscar. What would you like to **know** / **drink**?

Technology Connection: Email Headers

A **READ** the email. Circle the email addresses. Underline the date. Write a check (÷) next to the subject. Now answer this question:

What is the email about? _____

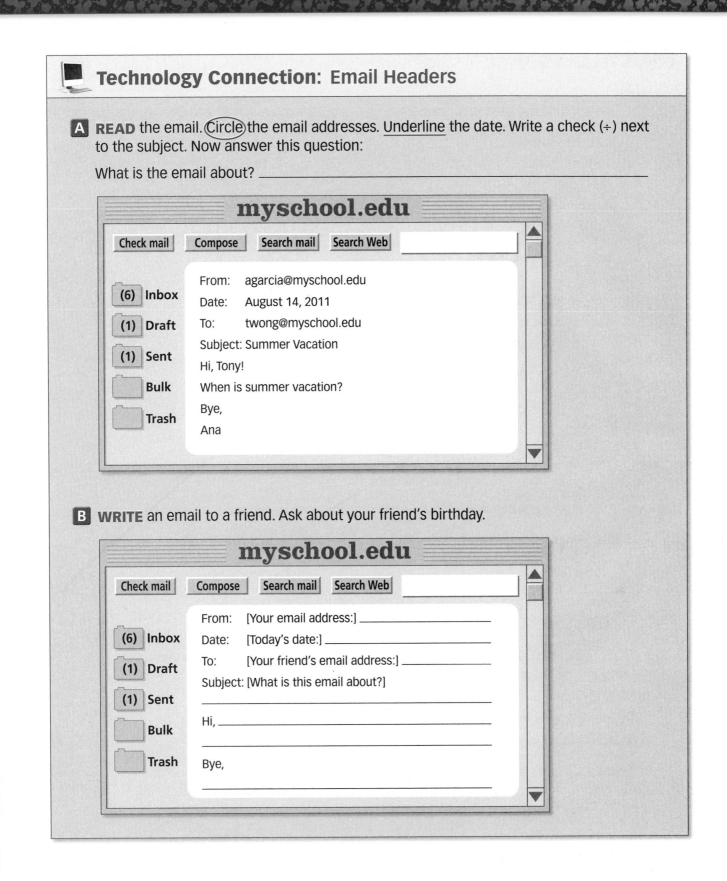

myschool.edu

| Check mail | Compose | Search mail | Search Web | |

(6) Inbox
(1) Draft
(1) Sent
Bulk
Trash

From: agarcia@myschool.edu
Date: August 14, 2011
To: twong@myschool.edu
Subject: Summer Vacation
Hi, Tony!
When is summer vacation?
Bye,
Ana

B **WRITE** an email to a friend. Ask about your friend's birthday.

myschool.edu

| Check mail | Compose | Search mail | Search Web | |

(6) Inbox
(1) Draft
(1) Sent
Bulk
Trash

From: [Your email address:] _____
Date: [Today's date:] _____
To: [Your friend's email address:] _____
Subject: [What is this email about?]
_____
Hi, _____
_____
Bye,
_____

Practice Test

LISTENING: Choose the best response. Then listen to the conversation and choose the correct answer.

1. What is her name?
   A. 12 Pine Street
   B. (924) 555-6857
   C. Her name is Sara.
   D. Good morning.

2. What does she look like?
   A. Thank you.
   B. Her name is Maria.
   C. She's tall and thin.
   D. She's in 8th grade.

3. What is the boy's name?
   A. Tony Ford
   B. Tony Lim
   C. Tony Way
   D. Way Lim

4. What is his address?
   A. 1333 Ford Way
   B. 3033 Ford Way
   C. 1333 4th Way
   D. 3033 4th Way

5. What grade is he in?
   A. 1st
   B. 3rd
   C. 4th
   D. 5th

GRAMMAR AND VOCABULARY. Choose the correct word or phrase to complete each sentence.

6. I _____ engaged.
   A. am
   B. is
   C. are
   D. have

7. They _____ twins.
   A. am
   B. is
   C. are
   D. has

8. She _____ short and thin.
   A. am
   B. is
   C. are
   D. has

9. _____ you in college?
   A. Are
   B. Is
   C. Have
   D. Where

10. _____ is summer vacation?
   A. Who
   B. When
   C. Is
   D. Where

11. _____ the classrooms?
   A. When is
   B. Who is
   C. Where are
   D. Where is

12. He's not married. He's _____.
   A. a twin
   B. my cousin
   C. single
   D. an adult

13. Alicia is my son's wife. She's my _____.
   A. daughter
   B. son-in-law
   C. daughter-in-law
   D. cousin

14. Tony and Jack aren't children. They're _____.
   A. adults
   B. single
   C. divorced
   D. widowed

15. Her hair isn't straight. It's _____.
   A. long
   B. tall
   C. short
   D. curly

16. There's no school December 15th to January 2nd. It's _____.
   A. elementary school
   B. the custodian
   C. the principal
   D. winter vacation

READING. Look at the flyer. Choose the correct answer.

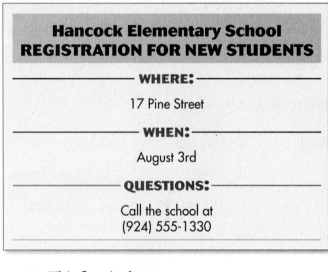

Hancock Elementary School
REGISTRATION FOR NEW STUDENTS

——————— **WHERE:** ———————
17 Pine Street

——————— **WHEN:** ———————
August 3rd

——————— **QUESTIONS:** ———————
Call the school at
(924) 555-1330

17. This flyer is about _____.
   A. registration for teachers
   B. summer vacation
   C. registration for old students
   D. registration for new students

18. The school is on _____.
   A. Pine Street
   B. August Street
   C. Hancock Street
   D. Elementary Street

19. Hancock is _____.
   A. an elementary school
   B. a high school
   C. a college
   D. an adult school

20. Registration is on _____.
   A. April 3rd
   B. August 3rd
   C. August 4th
   D. August 17th

UNIT 2 In the Community

Lesson 1

1 **MATCH** the pictures and the phrases. Write the letters.

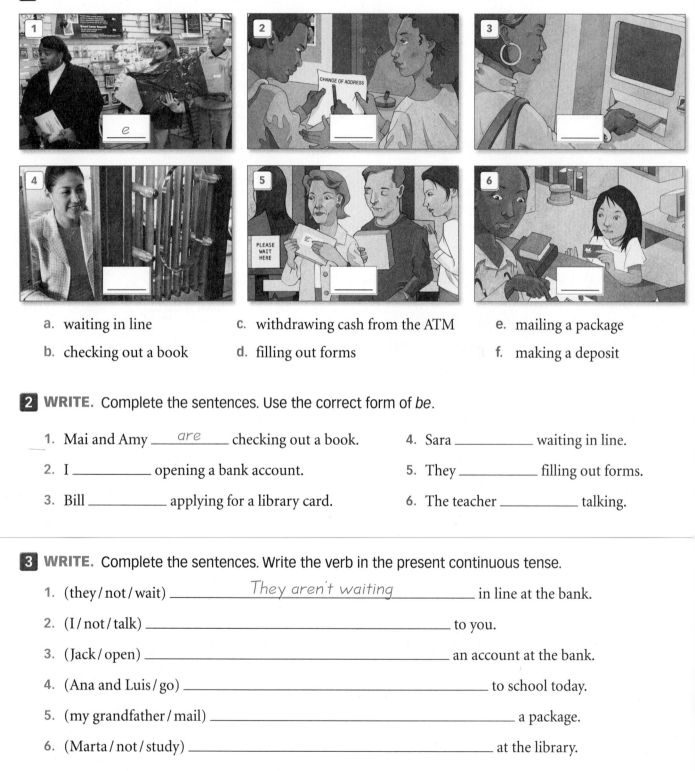

a. waiting in line

b. checking out a book

c. withdrawing cash from the ATM

d. filling out forms

e. mailing a package

f. making a deposit

2 **WRITE.** Complete the sentences. Use the correct form of *be*.

1. Mai and Amy ____are____ checking out a book.

2. I _____ opening a bank account.

3. Bill _____ applying for a library card.

4. Sara _____ waiting in line.

5. They _____ filling out forms.

6. The teacher _____ talking.

3 **WRITE.** Complete the sentences. Write the verb in the present continuous tense.

1. (they / not / wait) _____*They aren't waiting*_____ in line at the bank.

2. (I / not / talk) _____ to you.

3. (Jack / open) _____ an account at the bank.

4. (Ana and Luis / go) _____ to school today.

5. (my grandfather / mail) _____ a package.

6. (Marta / not / study) _____ at the library.

Lesson 2

1 WRITE. Complete the questions. Write the verb in the present continuous tense.

1. (he / wait) _____ Is he waiting _____ in line at the post office?

2. (Ana / study) What _____?

3. (she / buy) _____ stamps?

4. (Rob / go) Where _____?

5. (the teacher / say) What _____?

6. (you / go) When _____ to the mall?

2 MATCH the questions with the answers.

__c__ 1. What are Wei and Ping doing?   a. His books are overdue.

_____ 2. Is Sue waiting in line?   b. No, he isn't.

_____ 3. Are you making a deposit?   c. They're filling out forms.

_____ 4. Where is he going?   d. Yes, she is.

_____ 5. Why is Rob paying a late fee?   e. No, I'm not.

_____ 6. Is he going to the library with you?   f. To the post office.

3 WRITE. Complete the sentences with the words and phrases in the box.

an account	a deposit	a library card	a book	a form	a package	cash	in line

What's happening around the community today? It's busy at the bank. Jane is making

(1) _____ a deposit _____ . May and Chen are opening (2) _____. Outside, Matt

is withdrawing (3) _____ from the ATM. It's busy at the post office, too. Lots of

people are waiting (4) _____ . Sam is mailing (5) _____ . Alberto

and Ana are filling out (6) _____ . Over at the library, it's nice and quiet. Mike is

applying for (7) _____ , and Sue is checking out (8) _____ .

Lesson 3

1 LISTEN. Write the numbers under the pictures.

WCD, 12

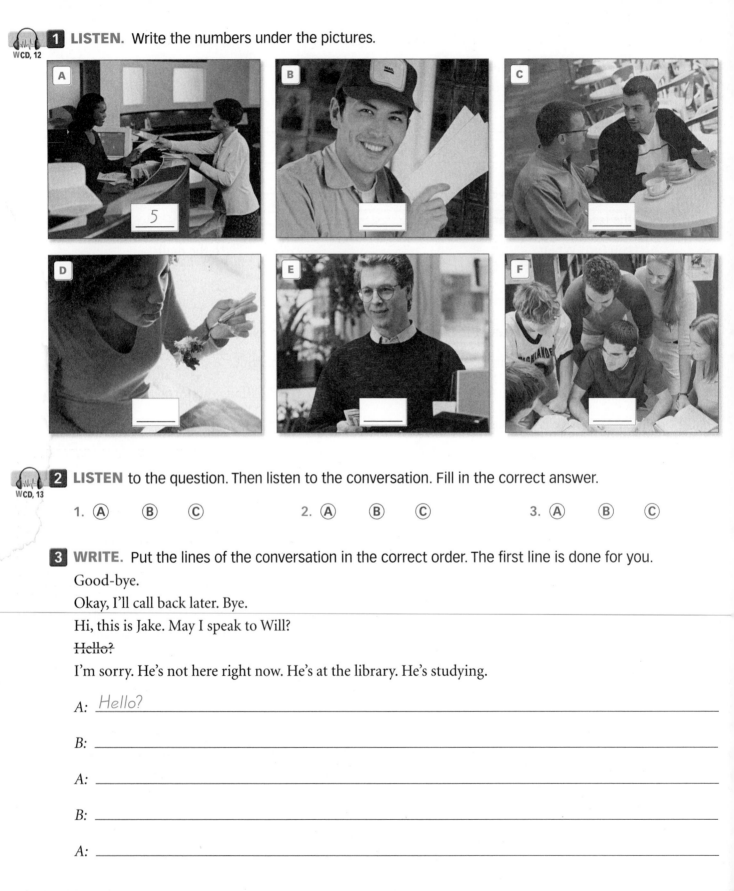

A   5

B   ___

C   ___

D   ___

E   ___

F   ___

2 LISTEN to the question. Then listen to the conversation. Fill in the correct answer.

WCD, 13

1. Ⓐ   Ⓑ   Ⓒ   2. Ⓐ   Ⓑ   Ⓒ   3. Ⓐ   Ⓑ   Ⓒ

3 WRITE. Put the lines of the conversation in the correct order. The first line is done for you.

Good-bye.

Okay, I'll call back later. Bye.

Hi, this is Jake. May I speak to Will?

~~Hello?~~

I'm sorry. He's not here right now. He's at the library. He's studying.

A: _Hello?_____

B: _____

A: _____

B: _____

A: _____

Culture and Communication — *Leaving Phone Messages*

1 **LISTEN** and read the conversations. Answer the questions. Then practice with a partner.

Ms. Brown: Hello?

Jane Smith: Hello. This is Jane Smith. May I please speak to Mr. Green?

Ms. Brown: I'm sorry. He's not available right now. Can he call you back?

Jane Smith: Yes. Thank you. My number is 555-6397.

---

1. Can Mr. Green speak to Jane now? **yes no**

2. How does Ms. Brown say this? Circle her words.

3. What does Jane say? Underline her words.

Sue: Hello?

Jane: Hi, Sue. It's Jane. Is Bob there?

Sue: No, he's not here right now. Can I take a message?

Jane: Sure. Tell him I called.

Sue: Okay, Jane.

---

1. Is Bob there? **yes no**

2. How does Sue say this? Circle her words.

3. What does Jane say? Underline her words.

---

2 **WRITE.** Complete the conversation. Use some sentences from the box.

A: Hello?

B: _____

A: _____

B: _____

Useful Expressions

When someone isn't there, say...

A: [I'm sorry.]

She's not here.

He can't come to the phone right now.

She's busy right now.

He's not available right now.

She'll be back later.

Can I take a message?

Can he call you later?

Can you call back later?

I'll have her call you.

I'll tell him you called.

B: Thank you.

Thanks.

My number is...

She can call me at...

Tell him I called.

Tell her...

---

3 **PRACTICE.** Now practice your conversation with a partner.

Lesson 4

1 MATCH the questions and answers.

___d___ 1. Can I pay with a check?

_____ 2. Can I exchange this sweater?

_____ 3. Would you like a plastic bag?

_____ 4. Could I get some change for this?

_____ 5. May I use this coupon?

_____ 6. May I help you?

a. Of course. May I see your receipt?

b. Sure. Here are four quarters.

c. I'm sorry. We don't accept coupons.

d. Sorry. We only accept cash.

e. Yes, please. I'd like to buy this shirt.

f. Paper, please.

2 WRITE. Unscramble the questions.

1. I / May / you / help / ? _May I help you?_____

2. a / paper bag / Could / I / have / ? _____

3. exchange / this / shirt / I / Can / ? _____

4. some / help / Would / like / you / ? _____

5. you / Can / the price/ tell / me / ? _____

6. pay / I / May / a check / with / ? _____

3 WRITE an answer for each question in Activity 2.

1. _Yes, please. Where are the sweaters?_____

2. _____

3. _____

4. _____

5. _____

6. _____

Lesson 5

1 LISTEN and circle the words you hear.

1. Could **you** / **I** have a paper bag?

2. Could **you** / **she** give me a receipt?

3. Could **you** / **he** call me later?

4. Could **you** / **she** tell me the price?

5. Could **you** / **I** exchange this?

6. Could **you** / **she** help me with this?

2 CIRCLE the words in the puzzle.

accept	account	cash	check	coupon	department	deposit	exchange
mail	overdue	pay	price	receipt	renew	return	

C	N	R	M	C	N	Y	T	Y	D	E	K	R	E	I
B	O	Y	E	N	A	P	A	E	E	X	C	Y	J	N
R	H	U	K	T	I	S	P	P	G	C	E	N	T	D
U	T	U	P	E	U	A	H	R	N	H	H	E	P	C
E	Z	I	C	O	R	R	A	V	A	A	C	B	C	T
U	U	E	S	T	N	J	N	A	H	N	T	Q	N	A
Y	R	D	M	O	N	R	M	N	C	G	P	U	R	C
N	V	E	R	R	P	O	H	F	O	E	O	Z	L	C
W	N	R	U	E	Q	E	U	P	D	C	Q	U	W	E
T	T	T	Z	W	V	E	D	L	C	C	H	T	F	P
P	R	I	C	E	Q	O	L	A	R	E	N	E	W	T
I	T	O	G	N	J	A	Y	J	P	Q	S	R	A	M
V	H	O	C	V	D	R	L	I	A	M	X	B	S	G
N	M	U	F	C	P	K	X	S	T	Y	J	L	T	T
W	G	W	A	C	C	O	U	N	T	L	S	D	J	W

Family Connection—*Getting a Library Card*

1 **READ** and look at the brochure.

Get a Pine Valley Library Card

What can I do with a library card?

- Borrow books, movies, and music CDs
- Use our computers
- Get library information from your home computer

How much is a library card?

A new library card is free.

How do I apply for a library card?

You must have one of these:
- A valid driver's license or passport with your current address

OR
- A photo ID plus a copy of a bill with your current name and address

Can my children get a library card?

Yes! Children under 16 years old need a parent
or guardian's signature to get a library card.

Congratulations! Now you have your card. What should you always remember?

- Take care of borrowed materials.
- Return materials on time.
- Pay late fees on time.
- Replace lost or damaged materials.

I lost my card. What should I do?

Tell the library immediately. There is a $1.00 fee to replace your card.

2 FIND AND MATCH. Find the words in the brochure. Then match the words with their meanings.

___b___ 1. bill
_____ 2. driver's license
_____ 3. passport
_____ 4. signature

a. it has your picture; you need it to travel to other countries
b. it tells you how much money to pay for things like electricity
c. your name in your handwriting
d. it has your picture; you need it to drive

3 CIRCLE *yes* or *no*.

1. With a library card, you can borrow movies.	(yes)	no
2. With a library card, you can use the library's computers.	yes	no
3. A new library card costs $1.00.	yes	no
4. You need a driver's license, passport, or a copy of a bill to get a library card.	yes	no
5. Children can get a library card.	yes	no
6. A 16-year-old girl can get her own library card.	yes	no
7. With a library card, you can keep materials as long as you want.	yes	no
8. It costs $10 to replace a lost library card.	yes	no

4 REAL-LIFE LESSON. Find out how to get a library card in your community. Put the information in the chart below.

What is the name of your library?	
What is the address of your library?	
What can you do with a library card?	
How much does it cost?	
How do you apply for a library card?	
How do children get library cards?	
When you get a card, what do you agree to do?	
What do you do if you lose your card?	
Do you have a library card?	

Community Connection—*Learning About Library Activities*

1 **READ** the flyer.

Pine Valley Library Activities

MONDAY	**Children** • **Preschool Story Time** Bring your children. Stories for ages 3–6. 10:00–10:30 A.M.
TUESDAY	**Children** • **Afternoon Story Time** Bring your children. Stories for ages 5–8. 3:30–4:00 P.M. **Adults** • **Email Basics Class** Learn how to set up an email account and read and send emails. 7:00–8:00 P.M.
WEDNESDAY	**Children** • **Preschool Story Time** Bring your children. Stories for ages 3–6. 10:00–10:30 A.M. **Adults** • **Book Club** Join us to discuss an interesting book. 7:00–8:00 P.M.
THURSDAY	**Children** •**Afternoon Story Time** Bring your children. Stories for ages 5–8. 3:30–4:00 P.M. **Adults** • **Internet Basics Class** Learn how to use a Web browser and how to use search engines. 7:00–8:00 P.M.
FRIDAY	**Teens** • **Computer Gaming/Pizza Party** Join other teens for pizza & computer activities. 6:00–8:00 P.M.

Hours: 9:00 A.M.–8:00 P.M. Monday–Saturday. Closed on Sunday.

Note: All activities are free.

2 **CIRCLE** the correct answer.

1. Preschool Story Time is for ages (3-6)/ 5-8.

2. Seven-year old children can hear stories at **10:00 A.M. / 3:30 P.M.**

3. Adults can learn about email on **Tuesday / Thursday.**

4. Adults can learn about the Internet on **Tuesday / Thursday.**

5. There is a book club for **adults / teens.**

6. There is a computer and pizza party for **adults / teens.**

7. There is a book club meeting on **Wednesday / Saturday.**

8. The Internet Basics Class **costs $5.00 / is free.**

3 **MATCH** the situations and the activities.

_b_ 1. Your 3-year-old son likes to listen to stories.

_____ 2. You want to learn about the Internet.

_____ 3. Your 7-year-old daughter wants something to do in the afternoons.

_____ 4. You want to talk about books with other adults.

_____ 5. Your mother wants to learn to send email.

_____ 6. You are a 14-year-old boy. You want to play computer games with other teens.

a. Computer Gaming/Pizza Party

b. Preschool Story Time

c. Email Basics Class

d. Afternoon Story Time

e. Internet Basics Class

f. Book Club

4 **REAL-LIFE LESSON.** At your library, what activities are for children, teens, and adults? Write the names of activities in the chart below.

Activities for . . .		
Children	**Teens**	**Adults**

Career Connection

1 **READ.** Oscar is looking at a college catalog.
Read the course descriptions.

Computer Courses

Course A – CS 108 (1 unit)
Introduction to Spreadsheets
Open to anyone.

Learn to use a personal computer spreadsheet software program
to design, create, and use spreadsheets for accounting and other
database applications.

Course number: 09453
11/27 - 12/15 – Sat. 9:10 - 11:30 A.M.
Meets in CS Building, Room 17 – Instructor: R. Ortiz

Course B – CS 118 (2 units)
Intermediate Spreadsheet Design
Prerequisite: All students must have taken CS 110

Techniques for designing business-oriented spreadsheets and
spreadsheet programming for custom applications.

Course number: 09461
10/18 - 12/13 – Thurs. 3:10 - 5:30 P.M.
Meets in CS Building, room 22 – Instructor: J. Hunt

2 **CIRCLE** *yes* or *no*.

1. Anyone can take Course B.	yes	(no)
2. Course A is on Saturdays.	yes	no
3. Course B is in the daytime.	yes	no
4. Course A is about 3 weeks long.	yes	no
5. Course B is about 3 weeks long.	yes	no
6. Course A is for people who know something about spreadsheets.	yes	no

3 **WRITE.** Circle your answer. Then give reasons.

Which course is best for Oscar? Circle your answer.   **Course A**   **Course B**

Why? List the reasons.

1. _____

2. _____

3. _____

4. _____

Technology Connection: Reading a College Website

A READ the Web page.

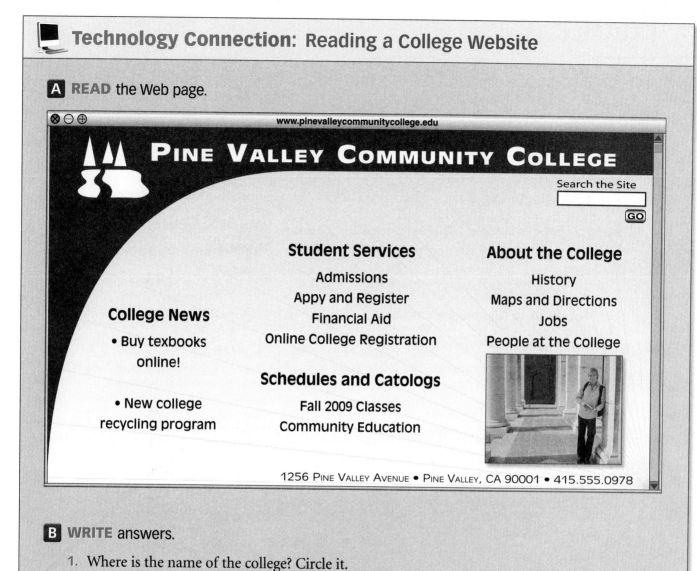

B WRITE answers.

1. Where is the name of the college? Circle it.

2. Where is the phone number of the college? Circle it.

3. What other kinds of information are on this Web page? _____

_____

4. You want to find out about a spreadsheet class for fall classes. What words do you click? Circle them.

5. You want to apply to Pine Valley Community College. What words do you click? Circle them.

6. You want to buy a textbook. What words do you click? Circle them.

Practice Test

WCD, 16

LISTENING. Choose the best response. Then listen to the conversation and choose the correct answer.

1. Hello?
   A. Good-bye.
   B. I'm sorry.
   C. She's not here right now.
   D. Hi. This is Laura.

2. May I speak to Luis?
   A. I'm sorry. He's not here right now.
   B. Hello?
   C. Good-bye.
   D. She wants to talk to Tony's mother.

3. Why is Ana calling?
   A. She wants to have lunch with Tony.
   B. She wants to talk to Tony.
   C. See wants to go to the cafe.
   D. She wants to talk to Tony's mother.

4. Where is Tony?
   A. at home
   B. at the cafe
   C. at Ana's house
   D. at his mother's house

5. What is Tony doing?
   A. working
   B. shopping
   C. eating
   D. studying

GRAMMAR AND VOCABULARY. Choose the correct word or phrase to complete each sentence.

6. She _____ a book.
   A. are checking out
   B. checking out
   C. is checking out
   D. checking

7. They _____ at the library.
   A. are studying
   B. is studying
   C. am studying
   D. studying

8. _____ he waiting in line?
   A. Am
   B. Is
   C. Are
   D. Has

9. _____ you doing?
   A. Are
   B. What are
   C. What is
   D. What am

10. *A:* Is he working today?
    B: No, he _____.
    A. is
    B. am
    C. aren't
    D. isn't

11. Could you _____ me?
    A. help
    B. helps
    C. helping
    D. is helping

32 | Unit 2

12. He's at the bank. He's making _____.
   A. a deposit
   B. a book
   C. a package
   D. in line

13. Alicia's at the post office. She's filling out a _____.
   A. late fee
   B. package
   C. cash
   D. form

14. Tony's at the library. He's applying for a _____.
   A. deposit
   B. late fee
   C. package
   D. library card

15. Your library book is overdue. Now you are paying a _____.
   A. late fee
   B. receipt
   C. store credit
   D. cash

16. You don't have cash. You are paying with _____.
   A. a receipt
   B. a credit card
   C. an ATM
   D. sales tax

READING. Read the email. Choose the correct answer.

FROM: Tom Smith
TO: Ann Green
SENT: February 11, 12:30 P.M.
SUBJECT: Hi

Hi Ann,

I'm thinking about you! I'm at school today. I'm checking my email. I'm with Sam and Tony. Sam is at the cafeteria. He's eating lunch. Tony is at the library. He's checking out a book.

What are you doing today? Are you at home? Can you have dinner with me at the mall tonight? Can you call me soon?

I miss you!
Tom

17. This email is to _____.
   A. Tom
   B. Sam
   C. Tony
   D. Ann

18. What is the main idea of the email?
   A. Tom, Sam, and Tony are doing things at school today.
   B. Tom, Sam, and Tony are doing things at the library today.
   C. Tom and Ann are doing things at school today.
   D. Tom and Ann are eating lunch at the cafeteria today.

19. Sam is _____.
   A. at the library
   B. at the cafeteria
   C. at home
   D. at the mall

20. Tony is _____.
   A. eating lunch
   B. checking email
   C. eating dinner
   D. checking out a book

UNIT 3 Daily Activities

Lesson 1

1 **MATCH** the pictures and the phrases. Write the letters.

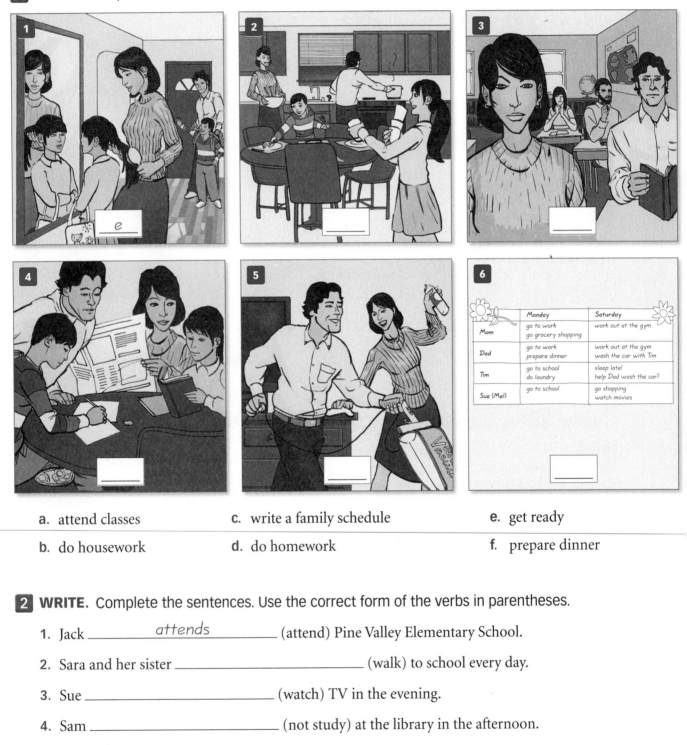

	Monday	Saturday
Mom	go to work go grocery shopping	work out at the gym
Dad	go to work prepare dinner	work out at the gym wash the car with Tim
Tim	go to school do laundry	sleep late! help Dad wash the car?
Sue (Me!)	go to school	go shopping watch movies

a. attend classes

b. do housework

c. write a family schedule

d. do homework

e. get ready

f. prepare dinner

2 **WRITE.** Complete the sentences. Use the correct form of the verbs in parentheses.

1. Jack _____*attends*_____ (attend) Pine Valley Elementary School.

2. Sara and her sister _____ (walk) to school every day.

3. Sue _____ (watch) TV in the evening.

4. Sam _____ (not study) at the library in the afternoon.

5. I _____ (not check) my email every day.

6. They _____ (buy) lunch in the cafeteria on Mondays.

Lesson 2

1 **WRITE.** Look at the schedule. Complete the paragraph with the correct form of the verbs in the chart.

	Monday	Saturday
Mom	go to work go grocery shopping	work out at the gym
Dad	go to work prepare dinner	work out at the gym wash the car with Tim
Tim	go to school do laundry	sleep late! help Dad wash the car?
Sue (Me!)	go to school	go shopping watch movies

Smith Family Routines

Monday and Saturday are very different days in our house! Monday is a busy day. On Monday, Mom and Dad (1) _____go_____ to work and Tim and I (2) _____ to school. After work, Mom (3) _____ grocery shopping. Dad (4) _____ dinner and Tim (5) _____ the laundry. Saturday isn't so busy. We all relax. Mom and Dad (6) _____ at the gym. Tim (7) _____ late. Dad (8) _____ the car, and sometimes Tim (9) _____ Dad. I go shopping and (10) _____ movies with my friends.

2 **WHAT ABOUT YOU?** Write sentences about your activities.

On Monday . . .

1. I _____

2. I _____

3. I _____

On Saturday . . .

4. I _____

5. I _____

6. I _____

Lesson 3

1 LISTEN. Circle the sound for the final *s*.

1.	*s*	*z*	(*iz*)	6.	*s*	*z*	*iz*
2.	*s*	*z*	*iz*	7.	*s*	*z*	*iz*
3.	*s*	*z*	*iz*	8.	*s*	*z*	*iz*
4.	*s*	*z*	*iz*	9.	*s*	*z*	*iz*
5.	*s*	*z*	*iz*	10.	*s*	*z*	*iz*

2 LISTEN to the phone calls. Number the appointment cards.

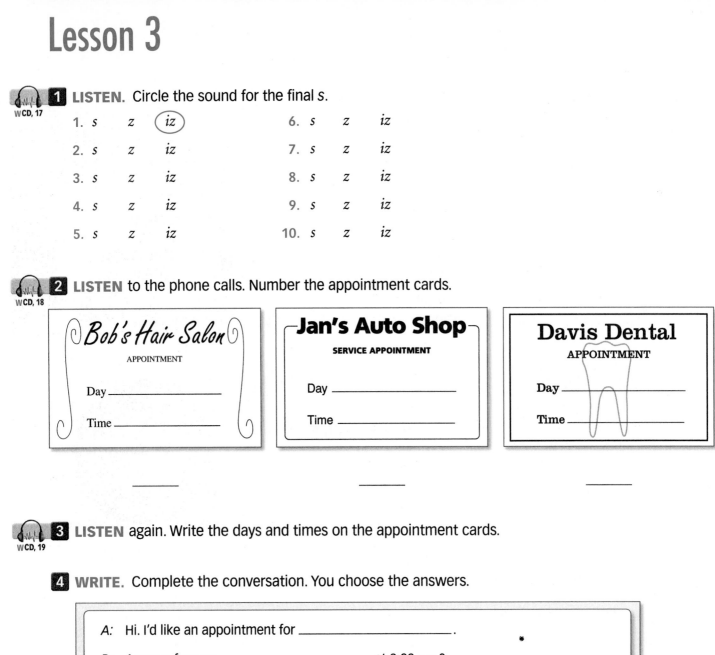

Bob's Hair Salon

APPOINTMENT

Day _____

Time _____

——————

Jan's Auto Shop

SERVICE APPOINTMENT

Day _____

Time _____

——————

Davis Dental

APPOINTMENT

Day _____

Time _____

——————

3 LISTEN again. Write the days and times on the appointment cards.

4 WRITE. Complete the conversation. You choose the answers.

A: Hi. I'd like an appointment for _____ .

B: Are you free on _____ at 8:00 A.M.?

A: Oh, I'm sorry. I _____ on _____ at 8:00 A.M.

B: Can you come on _____ at 8:00 A.M.?

A: Sure, that's fine.

Culture and Communication — *Excuses for Being Late*

1 **LISTEN** to and read the conversation. Look at the clock. Then practice the conversation with a partner.

Receptionist:	Davis Dental.
Ann:	Hi, this is Ann Smith. I'm very sorry. I'm going to be late for my appointment. I missed the bus.
Receptionist:	When will you be here?
Ann:	In about ten minutes.
Receptionist:	That's okay. Thanks for calling.

<table>
<tr><th colspan="2">Useful Expressions</th></tr>
<tr><td colspan="2">Excuses for Being Late</td></tr>
<tr><td>Apology</td><td>Excuse</td></tr>
<tr><td>I'm sorry. I'm going to be late for . . . because . . .</td><td>I missed the bus.
I'm having car trouble.
There's a lot of traffic today.
I got lost.
I couldn't find a parking place.</td></tr>
</table>

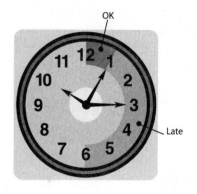

2 **WRITE.** Complete the conversations.

1. *Receptionist:* Lee's Beauty Shop.

   You: Hi, this is _____. I'm very sorry. I'm going to be late.

   _____.

   Receptionist: When will you be here?

   You: _____.

2. *Receptionist:* Mr. Green's Office.

   You: Hi, this is _____. I'm very sorry. I'm going to be late.

   _____.

   Receptionist: When will you be here?

   You: _____.

3 **PRACTICE.** Now practice your conversations with a partner.

Lesson 4

1 **MATCH** the sentences that mean the same.

   _d_   1. I don't work out at the gym.

         2. I work out at the gym every day.

         3. I work out at the gym once a year.

         4. I work out at the gym three times a month.

         5. I work out at the gym five times a week.

a. I sometimes work out at the gym.

b. I rarely work out at the gym

c. I usually work out at the gym.

d. I never work out at the gym.

e. I always work out at the gym.

2 **WRITE.** Unscramble the sentences.

1. English / every / Sam / speaks / day / . _Sam speaks English every day._

2. her email / checks / a day / Jane / three times / . _____

3. at / I / a snack / rarely / have / break time / . _____

4. She / at / studies / every / the library / day / . _____

5. sometimes / works out / Ana / the gym / at / . _____

6. the teacher / talks / Sue / usually / class / to / after / . _____

3 **WHAT ABOUT YOU?** Write sentences. Use *always, usually, sometimes, rarely, never* or other expressions of frequency.

1. (work out at the gym) _____

2. (speak English) _____

3. (send text messages) _____

4. (do laundry) _____

5. (go grocery shopping) _____

6. (prepare dinner) _____

Lesson 5

WCD, 21

1 **LISTEN** and number the pictures.

A ____5____

B _____

C _____

D _____

E _____

F _____

2 **WHAT ABOUT YOU?** Write sentences. Use *always, usually, sometimes, rarely, never* or other expressions of frequency.

1. (practice with a partner) _____

2. (come to class on time) _____

3. (have a test) _____

4. (look up words in the dictionary) _____

3 **READ** and complete the graph.

What do Pine Valley Adult School students do to relax? The Pine Valley newspaper asked this question. 675 students answered. 200 students reported that they check email. 150 students reported that they watch TV. 125 students watch movies, and 100 students listen to music. 75 students read, and only 25 work out at the gym.

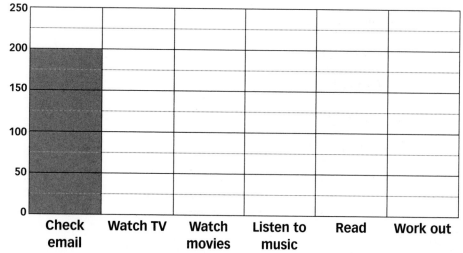

Family Connection—*Planning Family Chores*

1 **READ** the conversation.

Dad: So, kids, it's time for the family meeting. . . .

All Kids: Okay!

Mom: Ready. We have a lot of housework, and we'll all have jobs.

Sam: What's my job?

Mom: Just a minute . . . Let's look at the list. Jake, please read the list.

Jake: Okay. Here it is: Do laundry, prepare dinner, do ironing, set the table, go shopping, vacuum, and dust.

Sara: Don't forget: wash the car!

Dad: Right, Sara, thank you.

Mom: Now, let's decide: Who does each job?

Green Family Housework Chart					
	Dad	**Mom**	**Jake**	**Sam**	**Sara**
Go shopping		✓			
Do laundry	✓			✓	
Wash the car	✓				✓
Prepare dinner		✓	✓		
Do ironing			✓		
Set the table					✓
Vacuum	✓				
Dust				✓	

2 **WRITE** sentences about the Green Family Job Chart.

1. (Dad and Sam) _Dad and Sam do laundry._ _____

2. (Dad and Sara) _____

3. (Dad) _____

4. (Mom) _____

5. (Mom and Jake) _____

6. (Jake) _____

7. (Sam) _____

8. (Sara) _____

3 **REAL-LIFE LESSON.** Make a job chart for your family or for the people you live with. Have a meeting. Make a job list. Decide who will do each job.

Jobs	Name _____	Name _____	Name _____	Name _____	Name _____

Community Connection—*Getting Information About Your Community*

1 **READ** and look.

Andy: Hey, Bob. How are you?

Bob: Great. What's new?

Andy: I need an appointment for an eye exam. Do you know a good eye doctor?

Bob: Sure. I go to Dr. Honda. She's great.

Andy: Sounds good. Do you have her phone number?

Bob: I'll get it for you.

Andy: Thanks, Bob. I appreciate your help.

Bob: My pleasure.

2 **MATCH** the service and the person or place.

Service	Person / Place
_d_ 1. a (medical) check up	a. auto shop
_____ 2. an eye exam	b. dentist
_____ 3. a dental exam	c. carpet cleaning company
_____ 4. a haircut	d. doctor
_____ 5. some car repairs	e. eye doctor
_____ 6. a carpet cleaning	f. hair salon

3 **COMPLETE** the sentences. Use the words and phrases in Activity 2.

1. I need an appointment for _a check up_ .

   Do you know a good _doctor_ ?

2. I need an appointment for _____ .

   Do you know a good _____ ?

3. I need an appointment for _____ .

   Do you know a good _____ ?

4. I need an appointment for _____ .

   Do you know a good _____ ?

5. I need an appointment for _____ .

   Do you know a good _____ ?

6. I need an appointment for _____ .

   Do you know a good _____ ?

4 **TAKE IT OUTSIDE.** Ask family and friends to tell you about good services in the community. Complete the chart.

Family Member/Friend	Service	Phone Number

Career Connection—*Computer Calendars*

1 MATCH the days of the week and the short forms.

_d_ 1. Sunday   a. Wed

_____ 2. Monday   b. Fri

_____ 3. Tuesday   c. Sat

_____ 4. Wednesday   d. Sun

_____ 5. Thursday   e. Mon

_____ 6. Friday   f. Tue

_____ 7. Saturday   g. Thur

2 READ. Oscar usually works from 8:00 A.M. to 5:00 P.M. Monday to Friday. Read the appointments and activities on his computer calendar.

CALENDAR ⊗ ⊖ ⊕

October

2009

Today

Calendar

Options

Formats

To Do

Special dates

Time	Sunday 5	Monday 6	Tuesday 7	Wednesday 8	Thursday 9	Friday 10	Saturday 11
8:00 A.M.		office meeting					
9:00						meeting w/Lena	
10:00						meeting w/servers	
11:00							
12:00 P.M.			lunch w/ Marcos		lunch w/ Sam		
1:00							
2:00				dentist appointment			
3:00							wash car
4:00							
5:00							
6:00		pick up kids from soccer		pick up kids from soccer			Sara's birthday party
7:00							
8:00							
9:00							
10:00							

3 CIRCLE *yes* or *no*.

1. Oscar has a dentist appointment on Tuesday afternoon.   **yes**   (**no**)

2. Sara's birthday party is October 10.   **yes**   **no**

3. Oscar has a meeting on Monday, October 6.   **yes**   **no**

4. Oscar picks up the kids on Friday.   **yes**   **no**

5. Oscar has lunch with Marcos at 12 noon on Thursday.   **yes**   **no**

6. Oscar has one meeting on Friday.   **yes**   **no**

4 WRITE. Oscar wants to take a computer class. There are four classes:

> **Class A:** Monday, 6:00 P.M. to 8:00 P.M.
>
> **Class B:** Monday, 9:00 A.M. to 12 noon
>
> **Class C:** Tuesday, 6:00 P.M. to 8:00 P.M.
>
> **Class D:** Saturday, 9:00 A.M. to 12 noon

Which classes can Oscar take? Which class is the best? Explain your answer to a partner. Then write the best class on Oscar's calendar.

Technology Connection: Using a Computer Calendar

A WRITE. Number the steps for adding an appointment to Oscar's computer calendar.

To add an appointment on a computer calendar:

_____ Write in the name of the person or event.

___1___ Choose the day (date).

_____ Drag it to the time to end.

_____ Put the cursor on the time to begin.

_____ Add other notes.

B MATCH. Oscar can put his calendar appointments and activities into categories. Match the categories and the appointments.

___c___ 1. pick kids up from soccer   a. personal

_____ 2. office meeting   b. health

_____ 3. dentist appointment   c. family

_____ 4. Sara's birthday party   d. work

Practice Test

LISTENING: Choose the best response. Then listen to the conversation and choose the correct answer.

1. Hi, I'd like an appointment for a check up.
   A. Can you come Tuesday afternoon?
   B. Great. Thanks.
   C. Oh, I'm sorry.
   D. I attend classes on Tuesday.

2. Can you come on Wednesday morning?
   A. I need an appointment for some car repairs.
   B. Can you come in on Tuesday at 8:00 a.m.?
   C. Sorry. I have a dentist appointment on Wednesday morning.
   D. Thanks for the information.

3. Who does the man call?
   A. a dentist
   B. a doctor
   C. a friend
   D. an auto shop

4. What day is the appointment for car repairs?
   A. today
   B. Tuesday
   C. Thursday
   D. Monday

5. What time is the appointment for car repairs?
   A. 8:00 A.M.
   B. 8:15 A.M.
   C. 10:00 A.M.
   D. 11:00 A.M.

GRAMMAR AND VOCABULARY. Choose the correct word or phrase to complete each sentence.

6. She _____ the children ready for school every day.
   A. get
   B. gets
   C. getting
   D. are getting

7. He _____ the children every afternoon.
   A. pick up
   B. picks up
   C. pick ups
   D. picking up

8. They _____ school on Saturday.
   A. don't attend
   B. doesn't attend
   C. attends
   D. not attending

9. Maria _____ TV in the evening.
   A. doesn't watch
   B. watching
   C. don't watch
   D. not watching

10. Jack _____ the car on Saturday.
    A. usually washes
    B. washes usually
    C. usually washing
    D. usually wash

11. I _____ .
    A. every day study
    B. every day studies
    C. study every day
    D. studies every day

12. I'm studying at the library. I always do _____ there.
    A. homework
    B. housework
    C. laundry
    D. dinner

13. It's time for dinner. Dave always _____ the table.
    A. takes
    B. makes
    C. goes
    D. sets

14. Tony doesn't always exercise at home. Sometimes he _____ at the gym.
    A. drops out
    B. works out
    C. figures out
    D. checks out

15. I exercise at the gym every day. I _____ exercise there.
    A. never
    B. sometimes
    C. always
    D. usually

16. I'm never late for school. I'm always _____.
    A. in time
    B. on time
    C. miss
    D. sleep late

READING. Read the paragraph. Choose the correct answer.

> Monday is a busy day. I attend my English class from 8:00 A.M. to 12 NOON. In the afternoon, I go to work. I work from 12:30 P.M. to 5:30 P.M. At 6:00 P.M., I pick up my children from soccer. We eat dinner at 7:00 P.M.. In the evening, I help the children with their homework. At 9:00 P.M., I do my homework. At 11:00 P.M., I'm tired, and I go to bed.
>
> -Ana Martinez

17. What is the paragraph about?
    A. routines
    B. homework
    C. ESL classes
    D. weather

18. A good title for this paragraph is _____.
    A. A Fun Day
    B. My Saturday Routine
    C. A Usual Tuesday
    D. A Busy Day

19. When does Ana attend the English class?
    A. in the morning
    B. in the afternoon
    C. in the evening
    D. at 12:30 P.M.

20. What does Ana do in the evening?
    A. housework
    B. homework
    C. laundry
    D. shopping

UNIT 4 Finding a Job

LESSON 1

1 **MATCH** the questions and answers.

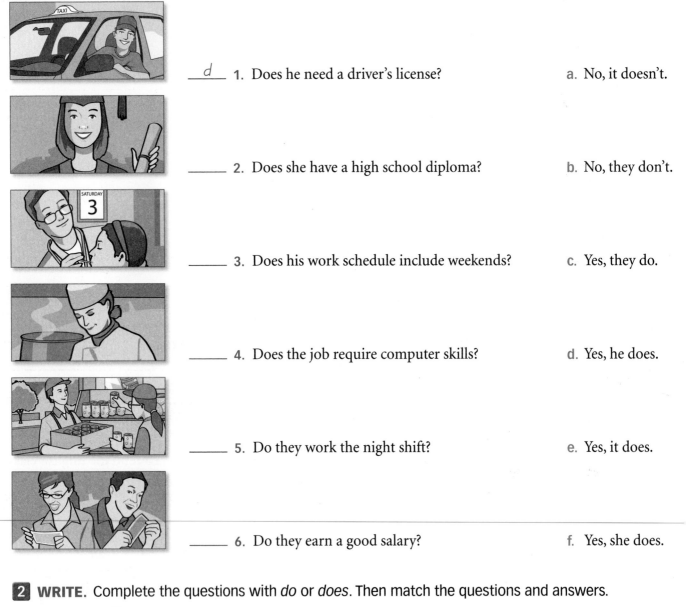

_____d_____ 1. Does he need a driver's license?   a. No, it doesn't.

_____ 2. Does she have a high school diploma?   b. No, they don't.

_____ 3. Does his work schedule include weekends?   c. Yes, they do.

_____ 4. Does the job require computer skills?   d. Yes, he does.

_____ 5. Do they work the night shift?   e. Yes, it does.

_____ 6. Do they earn a good salary?   f. Yes, she does.

2 **WRITE.** Complete the questions with *do* or *does*. Then match the questions and answers.

___e___ 1. _Do_ you have computer skills?   a. Yes, it does. She's a truck driver.

_____ 2. _____ her job require a driver's license?   b. No, they don't. They work the night shift.

_____ 3. _____ they work the day shift?   c. Yes, they do. They help the doctors.

_____ 4. _____ his work schedule include nights?   d. No, he doesn't. His pay is low.

_____ 5. _____ Leon earn a good salary?   e. Yes, I do. I use spreadsheets.

_____ 6. _____ they assist with patients?   f. Yes, it does. He works from 6:00 P.M. to 2:00 A.M.

LESSON 2

1 **WRITE** the questions. Use *do* or *does.* Then write the correct short answers.

1. *A:* (pilots/sweep and vacuum) _Do pilots sweep and vacuum_ ?
   B: _No, they don't._

2. *A:* (servers/serve food in restaurants) _____
   _____ ?
   B: _____

3. *A:* (flight attendants/help passengers during flights) _____
   _____ ?
   B: _____

4. *A:* (gardeners/inspect luggage) _____ ?
   B: _____

5. *A:* (cashiers/collect money and make change) _____
   _____ ?
   B: _____

6. *A:* (airport security agents/take care of plants) _____
   _____ ?
   B: _____

2 **READ AND WRITE.** Read the sentences about the people. Write their job responsibilities.
Use the correct form of the phrases in the box.

serve food in restaurants	fly airplanes	collect money and make change
take care of plants	supervise workers	help passengers during flights

1. Lee is a flight attendant. He _helps passengers during flights_ .

2. Marta is a pilot. She _____ .

3. Sara is a gardener. She _____ .

4. Jane and Jake are servers. They _____ .

5. Rob is a manager. He _____ .

6. Sue and Sam are cashiers. They _____ .

LESSON 3

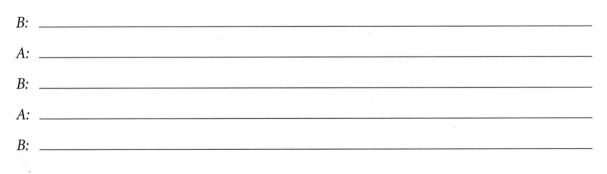

1 LISTEN. Circle the words you hear.

1. Does **he** / **she** fly airplanes?
2. Does **he** / **she** assist with patients?
3. Does **he** / **she** earn a good salary?
4. Does **he** / **she** inspect luggage?
5. Does **he** / **she** collect money?
6. Does **he** / **she** sweep and vacuum?
7. Does **he** / **she** supervise workers?
8. Does **he** / **she** work the day shift?

2 LISTEN to the question. Then listen to the conversation. Fill in the correct answer.

1. Ⓐ   Ⓑ   Ⓒ
2. Ⓐ   Ⓑ   Ⓒ
3. Ⓐ   Ⓑ   Ⓒ

3 WRITE. Put the lines of the conversation in the correct order. The first line is done for you.

Yes, I do. I have five years' experience.

I'm looking for a job as an airport security agent.

~~What kind of job are you looking for?~~

I'm looking for a full-time job.

Do you have experience?

Do you want a full-time job or part-time job?

A: *What kind of job are you looking for?* _____

B: _____

A: _____

B: _____

A: _____

B: _____

Culture and Communication—*Discussing Skills and Experience*

1 **LISTEN** to and read the conversation. Look at the picture. Then practice the conversation with a partner.

WCD, 25

Ms. Davis:	So, Ann, tell me about yourself.
Ann:	Well, I have three years' experience in sales. I have a college degree in business. I also have excellent computer skills.
Ms. Davis:	Okay. Uhmm, now tell me: why do you want this job?
Ann:	Ford Fashions is a good company to work for. Also, I think my sales experience can help the company.
Ms. Davis:	All right, then. Thank you for coming in.
Ann:	Thank you, Ms. Davis.

2 **WRITE.** Answer the questions about the conversation and picture.

1. What does Ann say about herself? Circle her words.

2. What does Ann say about Ford Fashions? Circle her words.

3. Can Ann help the company? Underline her words.

Useful Expressions:	
Typical Interview Questions	**Possible Answers**
Tell me about yourself.	Talk about: • years of experience • degrees and certificates • other skills
Why do you want to work here?	Say good things about the company. Talk about how you can help the company.

3 **WRITE.** Think about an interview. Think of a job and a company. What will you wear?

Job: _____ Company: _____

I will wear _____

What will you say? Complete the conversation.

Interviewer: Tell me about yourself.

You: _____

Interviewer: Why do you want to work here?

You: _____

4 **PRACTICE.** Now practice your conversation with a partner.

LESSON 4

1 WRITE. Complete the questions with *do* or *does*. Then match the questions and answers.

__f__ 1. Where __do__ you work?

_____ 2. When _____ he go home?

_____ 3. What benefits _____ they offer?

_____ 4. How much _____ you pay for overtime?

_____ 5. How _____ she get to work?

_____ 6. Why _____ he need a car?

_____ 7. Who _____ I work with?

_____ 8. Where _____ they take a break?

a. Because the job site is not near his house.

b. You work with Sam.

c. We pay $15.00 an hour for overtime.

d. In the employee lounge.

e. He goes home at 5:30 P.M.

f. I work at the airport.

g. They offer health insurance.

h. She takes the bus.

2 WRITE. Unscramble the questions.

1. What / does / do / the company / ? _What does the company do?_____

2. benefits / the company / offer / Does / ? _____

3. the union / do / does / What / ? _____

4. take / the employees / Where / a break / do / ? _____

5. I / apply / do / How / ? _____

6. get / How / overtime / for / much / he / does / ? _____

3 LISTEN and number the pictures.

WCD, 26

A   5

B

STATE CERTIFICATE
This certifies that
Jinn Kwan
Has successfully met the requirements of
General Equivalency Diploma
On this _21st_ Day of _June_ 20 _10_
Dire_____

C

D

ours	
Regular Hours	40 at $11.00 per hr
Overtime Hours	6 at $15.75 per hr
Pay	
Total regular pay	
Total overtime pay	
Total Earned	
Deductions (taxes, health insurance)	
Total Pay for Wee	

E

WORKERS UNION OF AMERICA
A.F.L.-C.I.O.
SYSTEM
LOCAL 127
"LIVE BETTER
WORK UNION"
THIS CARD CERTIFIES THAT
ANTONIO SANCHEZ
is a Union member in good standing on Local 127
under check-off agreement
JOSH CONWAY   ROBERT SMITH
PRESIDENT   ARY–TREASURER

F

STATE LICENSING BOARD
HEALTH AND HUMAN SERVICES DEPARTMENT
THIS IS TO CERTIFY THAT
Amisha Chopra
is duly registered and entitled to practice as a
DAY CARE WORKER
Certificate of responsibility 04678
Expires 14 Nov. 2010
CHAIRMAN
SECRETARY

LESSON 5

1 WRITE. Complete the paragraph. Use the words in the box.

diploma	benefits	certificate	inspect	insurance
leave	pay	supervise	vacation	years

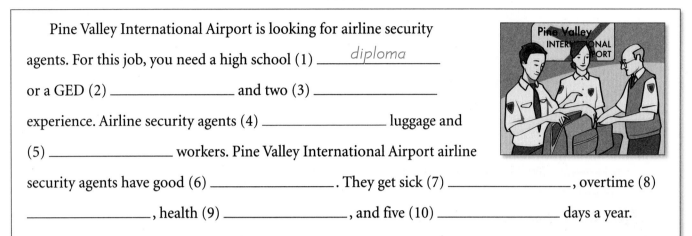

Pine Valley International Airport is looking for airline security agents. For this job, you need a high school (1) ___*diploma*___ or a GED (2) _____ and two (3) _____ experience. Airline security agents (4) _____ luggage and (5) _____ workers. Pine Valley International Airport airline security agents have good (6) _____. They get sick (7) _____, overtime (8) _____, health (9) _____, and five (10) _____ days a year.

2 WRITE. Complete the crossword puzzle.

ACROSS
4. a form you use to apply for a job
6. They supervise workers.
8. You need this to drive.

DOWN
1. Many jobs require a high school _____.
2. They take care of plants.
3. a place to rest at work
5. examples are vacation days and sick leave
7. another word for *pay*

3 WRITE. Do the math. Complete the pay stub with the correct numbers.

Pine Valley Natural Foods		
Employee name: Rob Taylor	Dates: Sept. 1 through Sept. 8	
Regular hours: 40 hours at $15.00 per hr.	Total regular pay	$_____
Overtime hours: 13 hours at $17.50 per hr.	Total overtime pay	+ $_____
	Total pay earned	$_____
	Deductions (taxes, health insurance)	– $137.40
	Total pay for week	$_____

Family Connection — *Reading a Course Catalog*

1 **READ** part of a community education course catalog.

Pine Valley Adult School – Community Education

- Do you want to learn new skills? Do you want to improve your skills?
- Do you need a degree or a certificate for your job?
- Do you want to prepare for a new career?
- Do you just want to have fun?

Pine Valley Adult School (PVAS) offers hundreds of courses—both in-class and online—including the following options:

Note: *means online course.

Computer Basics: Learn to use the Internet and email. Learn about word processing and spreadsheet programs.*

Computer Repair Certificate Program: Prepare for a career in computer repair. Learn to repair, install, and maintain computers.*

Construction Management: Are you a construction worker? Do you want to improve your skills and make more money? Become a manager! Learn how to manage construction projects and workers.

English as a Second Language, Grammar Review: A review of English grammar for intermediate-level students.

GED Preparation: Get your GED certificate fast! Practice in all the GED test areas: Writing, Social Studies, Science, Literature, and Math.*

Guitar: Learn to play the guitar! Beginners are welcome.

Resume Writing Workshop: Do you know how to write a resume that will get you a job? The Resume Writing Workshop will teach you everything you need to know.*

Veterinarian Assistant Certificate Program: Do you love animals? Would you like to work with animal doctors? The Veterinarian Assistant Program prepares you for a fun career.

Write Your Life Story: Learn how to tell the story of your life—for your friends, your children, and yourself!

2 **CIRCLE** *yes* or *no*.

1. The guitar class is online.	yes	**no**
2. The GED preparation class is online.	yes	no
3. The English as a Second Language class is for intermediate students.	yes	no
4. You can learn how to repair computers in Computer Basics.	yes	no
5. The Resume Writing Workshop teaches how to write your life story.	yes	no
6. The Resume Writing Workshop can help you get a job.	yes	no
7. You can learn how to be an animal doctor at PVAS.	yes	no
8. You can learn how to manage construction projects at PVAS.	yes	no

3 **WRITE.** Write the course names in the correct categories.

Computer Basics	~~Computer Repair Certificate Program~~	Construction Management
ESL, Grammar Review	GED Prep	Guitar
Resume Writing	Vet. Assistant Program	Write Your Life Story

Learn/ Improve Skills	Get a Degree/Certificate	Prepare for a Career/Job	Have Fun
	Computer Repair Certificate Program		

4 **READ** about the people. Use the information from Activity 3. Write the best course for each person.

1. Lisa is a construction worker. She likes her job, but she wants more pay and better benefits.
   Construction Management

2. Luis wants to prepare for a career, and he loves animals.
   _____

3. Marta wants to get a job, but she doesn't have a high school diploma.
   _____

4. Sam wants to apply for a job at a big company. He doesn't have a resume.
   _____

5. Ana speaks English well, but she sometimes forgets grammar rules.
   _____

6. Ana is looking for something fun to do, and she loves music.
   _____

5 **REAL-LIFE LESSON.** Get a catalog for an adult school or a community education program.

Name of School:			
Learn/ Improve Skills	Get a Degree/Certificate	Prepare for a Career/Job	Have Fun

Community Connection—*Writing a Résumé*

1 READ about Teresa.

Teresa wants a job as a childcare assistant. She is writing a **résumé**. It tells employers about her work experience and education.

5932 Landis Street   Phone: (619) 555-4893
San Diego, CA 92105   E-mail: Tgomez61@mail.com

Teresa L. Gomez

Objective	To obtain a position as a child care assistant.
Experience	*Teacher's Assistant* - January 2005 – Present
	Lincoln Elementary School, Chula Vista, CA
	• Assisted in planning daily activities
	• Prepared materials and set up learning areas
	• Supervised the classroom
	Salesperson - February 1999 – March 2003
	Maria Bonita Clothing Shop, Mexico City, Mexico
	• Assisted customers
	• Used cash register
	• Unpacked and displayed merchandise
Education	Chula Vista Community College - Childcare Certificate
	Liceo Chapultepec - High School Diploma
Skills	Speak fluent Spanish
	Play guitar
References	Available upon request.

---

2 CIRCLE the correct words.

1. Teresa's resume includes her **phone number / age**.

2. Teresa's resume **does / does not** include information about her family.

3. An *objective* is the job Teresa **has now / wants**.

4. The **Experience / Skills** section of Teresa's resume shows her past job responsibilities.

5. The **Education / Experience** section of Teresa's resume lists her schools.

6. Teresa has a **GED / Childcare** certificate.

7. Teresa has **music / computer skills**.

3 **WRITE.** Answer the questions about résumés.

1. What kind of information do you put in a résumé? _____
   _____

2. Do you put your age on a résumé? _____ Explain your answer. _____
   _____

3. Do you say that you are married on a résumé? _____ Explain your answer. _____
   _____

4. Do you include information about your children on résumé? _____ Explain your answer. _____
   _____

4 **WHAT ABOUT YOU?** Do you have any special skills? List them.

Computer skills: _____

Language skills: _____

Other skills: _____

5 **TAKE IT OUTSIDE.** Write a resume for a friend. Ask about your friend's objective, experience, education, and skills. Complete the form.

	Address:	Phone number:
		Email:
Name:		
Objective:		
Experience:		
Education:		
Skills:		
References:		

Career Connection—*Asking for Letters of Recommendation*

1 **READ** about Oscar.

Oscar is asking for a **letter of recommendation.** Oscar managed a big project at his son's school. The principal knows Oscar. She knows that Oscar is a good manager, so Oscar is calling her.

Jane: Hello?

Oscar: Hi, Jane, How are you?

Jane: Just fine. What's up, Oscar?

Oscar: Well, Jane, I'm applying for a new job.

Jane: Great! What kind of job?

Oscar: It's a management job.

Jane: Oscar, you're an excellent manager. I'm sure you'll get the job!

Oscar: Well, that's why I'm calling. Can you write me a letter of recommendation?

Jane: I'd be happy to. When do you need it?

Oscar: Oh, in about a week.

Jane: No problem.

2 **CIRCLE** the words to complete the sentences.

1. Oscar wants a **letter of recommendation** / **résumé**.

2. Oscar is asking **his mother** / **a school principal** for a letter of recommendation.

3. Oscar **managed a project at** / **went to** the school.

4. The principal **knows** / **does not know** Oscar.

5. Jane is **happy** / **unhappy** to help Oscar.

6. Oscar needs the letter **tomorrow** / **in about a week**.

3 **WRITE.** Answer the questions about letters of recommendation.

1. Is it a good idea to ask a relative to write a letter of recommendation? _____

2. Can you write your own letter of recommendation? _____

3. Today is March 1st. You need a letter of recommendation by March 15th. When do you start asking people for letters? _____

4. Who knows your work? Make a list of at least three people you can ask for a letter of recommendation.

   _____

Technology Connection: Finding Jobs Online

A **MATCH** the words and the examples.

_d_ 1. a keyword

a. ⟨ **Search for a Job!** ▼ ⟩

_____ 2. a job category

b. Airlines, Computers, Healthcare

_____ 3. a job location

c. Montgomery, Alabama; Miami, Florida

_____ 4. a pull-down menu

d. an important word; it helps you find information online

B **WRITE.** Look at part of a job search Web page. Then number the steps for looking for a job online.

Job Searcher: [_____]
Keywords (e.g., healthcare, construction)

| Category – Select ▲▼ |

| Job Location – Select ▲▼ |

_____ Select a job location.

_4_ Click the "Job Location" pull-down menu.

_____ Click the "Job Category" pull-down menu.

_____ Write a keyword (a job title) in the textbox.

_____ Select a job category

C **WRITE.** Do a job search. Write the keyword (a job title). Then write a job category and a job location for you.

Keyword: [_____]

Job Category: [_____]

Job Location: [_____]

Practice Test

LISTENING. Choose the best response. Then listen to the conversation and choose the correct answer.

1. What kind of job are you looking for?
   A. No, I don't.
   B. I have two years' experience.
   C. I attend classes on Wednesday morning.
   D. I'm looking for a job as a teacher.

2. Do you have experience?
   A. No, I work 8:00 A.M. to 5:00 P.M.
   B. Yes, I do. I have two years' experience.
   C. I want a full-time job.
   D. I'm calling about the assistant manager position.

3. What job does the man have?
   A. He's a cashier.
   B. He's a theater manager.
   C. He works on the weekends.
   D. He works part-time.

4. Where does the man work?
   A. on the weekends
   B. in the movies
   C. at a theatre
   D. full-time

5. When does the man work?
   A. full-time on weekdays
   B. part-time on weekdays
   C. part-time on weekends
   D. full-time on weekends

GRAMMAR AND VOCABULARY. Choose the correct word or phrase to complete each sentence.

6. _____ you work on weekends?
   A. Does
   B. Do
   C. When
   D. Doing

7. _____ Rob earn a good salary?
   A. Does
   B. Do
   C. Who
   D. Earn

8. *A:* Does she work part-time?
   B: No, she _____ .
   A. don't
   B. doesn't
   C. does
   D. do

9. _____ her job require computer skills?
   A. Do
   B. Don't
   C. Does
   D. How much

10. What benefits _____ the company offer?
    A. don't
    B. does
    C. doing
    D. do

11. You need a high school diploma or a GED _____ for this job.
    A. experience
    B. certificate
    C. benefits
    D. salary

12. _____ overtime does he get?
    A. When
    B. How
    C. How much
    D. Why

13. Managers _____ workers.
    A. fly
    B. sweep
    C. supervise
    D. collect

14. Gardeners _____.
    A. take care of plants
    B. help passengers during flights
    C. serve food
    D. fly airplanes

15. The company has good _____. They offer health insurance.
    A. overtime
    B. sick leave
    C. salary
    D. benefits

16. The _____ is good, too. I make $15.00 an hour.
    A. salary
    B. benefits
    C. sick leave
    D. insurance

READING. Read the job application. Choose the correct answer.

APPLICATION FOR EMPLOYMENT

PERSONAL INFORMATION

Name

Ruiz	Tony	L
Last	First	Middle Initial

Address	City	State	Zip Code
5932 Lincoln Street	Chicago	IL	60620

Phone no.	Email address
(312) 555-4893	Truiz@mail.com

Are you 18 years or older? __X__ Yes _____ No	Social Security Number 234-56-7890

Sex __X__ Male _____ Female	Do you have a driver's license? __X__ Yes _____ No	If yes, what state? IL

EMPLOYMENT

Position desired Flight attendant	Check one: __X__ Full–time ___ Part–time	When can you work? __X__ Day __X__ Night __X__ Weekends

EDUCATION: Years of school 0 1 2 3 4 5 6 7 8 9 10 11 ⑫ 13 14 15

WORK EXPERIENCE (Write current or most recent experience first.)

From	To	Employer	Position
Jan 2005	present	O'Hare International Airport	Airport Security Agent

17. How many years of school does Tony have?
    A. 12
    B. 234-56-7890
    C. 18
    D. Jan 2005

18. What job does Tony have now?
    A. Truiz@mail.com
    B. flight attendant
    C. O'Hare International Airport
    D. airport security agent

19. What job does Tony want?
    A. part-time
    B. weekends
    C. flight attendant
    D. airport security agent

20. When can Tony work?
    A. days, nights, and weekends
    B. part-time
    C. O'Hare International Airport
    D. Chicago

Lesson 1

1 **MATCH** the picture and the sentence.

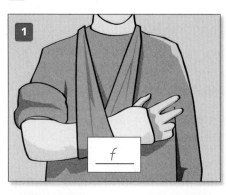

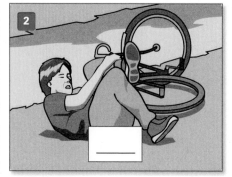

f

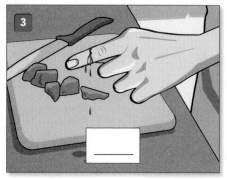

a. Sue cut her finger.

b. Jane sprained her wrist.

c. Martin broke his leg.

d. Maria and Luis went to the emergency room.

e. Irina got stitches.

f. John got a cast.

2 **CIRCLE** the correct form of the verb.

1. Tim **sprain / sprained** his ankle yesterday.

2. Sara **call / called** her mother last weekend.

3. He **broke / break** his arm last year.

4. Jin **cut / cuts** his finger yesterday.

5. The doctor **applying / applied** burn cream.

6. The child **burned / burning** her hand on the stove yesterday.

3 **WRITE** the past tense forms of the verbs.

1. walk _____walked_____

2. shop _____

3. play _____

4. try _____

5. want _____

6. dance _____

Lesson 2

1 WRITE the negative form of the verb.

1. Ana sprained her ankle. She _____*didn't break*_____ (not break) it.

2. Leon cut his finger. He _____ (not burn) it.

3. Jack and Jane went home. They _____ (not stay) at the hospital.

4. Lisa cut her finger, so she _____ (not apply) burn cream.

5. Luis went to the emergency room. He _____ (not go) to the doctor's office.

6. The doctor examined my leg, but she _____ (not put) a cast on it.

2 WRITE. Complete the sentences. Use the past form of the verb in parentheses.

1. Ann _____*hit*_____ (hit) her head and _____ (go) to the emergency room.

2. Bill _____ (fall) and _____ (break) his arm.

3. The children _____ (catch) a cold and _____ (feel) very sick.

4. Sam _____ (cut) his hand and _____ (get) stitches.

5. I _____ (eat) something bad and _____ (make) an appointment to see the doctor.

6. Jake _____ (break) his arm. It _____ (hurt) a lot. He _____ (take) some medicine and _____ (go) to sleep.

7. She _____ (examine) my arm.

8. The nurse _____ (fix) my bandage.

Lesson 3

1 **LISTEN.** Circle the sound for the final *-ed*.

WCD, 28

1.	(t)	d	id	6.	t	d	id
2.	t	d	id	7.	t	d	id
3.	t	d	id	8.	t	d	id
4.	t	d	id	9.	t	d	id
5.	t	d	id	10.	t	d	id

2 **LISTEN** to the question. Then listen to the conversation. Fill in the correct answer.

WCD, 29

1. Ⓐ Ⓑ Ⓒ

2. Ⓐ Ⓑ Ⓒ

3. Ⓐ Ⓑ Ⓒ

3 **WRITE.** Complete the conversation. Use the phrases in the box.

burned my hand	check it this week	how about Wednesday
make an appointment	Thank you	What's the problem

A: Pine Valley Medical Office. How may I help you?

B: My name is Marie Laval. I'd like to _____ .

A: _____ ?

B: I _____ last week. The doctor wanted to

_____ .

A: Which doctor do you see?

B: Dr. Sanchez.

A: Okay, _____ , June 17 at 10:30 A.M.?

B: That's fine. _____ .

A: We'll see you then.

B: Goodbye.

Culture and Communication—*Expressing Sympathy*

1 LISTEN to and read the conversation. Then practice the conversation with a partner.

Sue: Hello?

Ann: Hi, Sue. It's Ann. I can't come to work today.

Sue: What's the problem?

Ann: I fell yesterday, and I broke my arm.

Sue: Oh, I'm so sorry to hear that!

Ann: Thank you.

Sue: How are you doing?

Ann: I'm in a lot of pain.

Sue: Well, stay home and take it easy.

Ann: Okay.

Sue: I hope you feel better soon.

Ann: Thanks, Sue.

Useful Expressions

Ways to Express Sympathy

I'm sorry to hear that.	I hope you feel better soon.
What a shame!	I hope you'll be okay soon.
That's too bad.	Get well soon.
How are you doing?	Take it easy.
How are you feeling?	Take care of yourself.

2 CIRCLE *yes* or *no*.

1. Sue has a problem.   yes   (no)
2. Ann can come to work.   yes   no
3. Ann broke her arm.   yes   no
4. Ann is in a lot of pain.   yes   no
5. Sue wants to stay home and take it easy.   yes   no
6. Sue wants Ann to stay home.   yes   no

3 WRITE. Think about the situations. Write a response.

1. Your friend is sick. You say: _____

2. Your mother is in pain. You say: _____

3. Your co-worker sprained her ankle and can't come to work. You say: _____

4 PRACTICE. Choose a situation from Activity 3. Write a conversation. Practice your conversation with a partner.

Lesson 4

1 WRITE. Complete the sentences. Use the time expressions in the box.

last night	last week	last weekend	last year
the day before yesterday	this morning	two years ago	~~yesterday~~

1. I had a follow-up visit on Tuesday. I had a follow-up visit _____ *yesterday* _____.

2. Ana joined a gym on Saturday. She joined _____.

3. They went to the emergency room on Monday. That was _____
_____.

4. Sara lost 50 pounds in 2010. She lost the weight _____.

5. Leon went to the doctor at 8:00 A.M. on Wednesday, June 13, 2011.
He went to the doctor _____.

6. I called my mother at 8:00 P.M., June 12. I called her _____.

7. My son started high school in 2009. He started _____.

8. Jack had a heart attack on Wednesday, June 6. He had a heart attack _____.

2 WRITE. Unscramble the sentences.

1. year / last / Raul / high / pressure / had / blood / . _Raul had high blood pressure last year._
_____

2. months / Raul / six / went / the / doctor / to / ago / . _____
_____

3. ago / He / months / his / changed / five / diet / . _____
_____

4. last / Raul / gym / joined / a / week / . _____
_____

3 WHAT ABOUT YOU? Write answers to the questions.

1. What did you do this morning? _____

2. What did you do yesterday? _____

3. What did you do last weekend? _____

4. What did you do last year? _____

Lesson 5

1 **WRITE.** Put the words into the correct place in the chart.

allergies	antibiotics	antihistamines	asthma
blood pressure medication	cough	cough syrup	diabetes
~~earache~~	ear drops	headache	heart attack
high blood pressure	infection	~~inhaler~~	pain reliever

Medical Problems	Medications
earache	*inhaler*

2 **WRITE.** Complete the sentences. Use words and phrases from the chart.

1. Jane has _____ *diabetes* _____. She takes insulin.

2. Mark used his inhaler this morning. He has _____.

3. Isabel has a headache, so she took a/an _____.

4. Rob takes _____ because he has high blood pressure.

5. Tina took antibiotics because she has a/an _____.

6. Sam has allergies, so he took _____ this morning.

3 **WRITE.** Do the math. Read the label and answer the questions.

1. Marta took 1 pill at 3 P.M. What time can she take Pain Be Gone again? _____

2. Tim took 1 pill at 7 A.M. and 2 pills at 11:30 A.M. How many more pills can he take today? _____

3. John took 1 pill at 1 P.M., 2 pills at 4 P.M., and 1 pill at 8 P.M. How many more pills can he take today? _____

4. Jake took 2 pills at 10 A.M. and 2 pills at 2 P.M. When can he take more Pain Be Gone? _____

5. Sanjay took 1 pill at 9:30 A.M., 2 pills at 2 P.M., and 2 pills at 6 P.M. How many more can he take? _____

Pain Be Gone

Directions:
Adults and children over 12:
- Take 1 or 2 pills every 4 hours.
- Do not take more than 6 pills in 24 hours.

Children under 12: Ask a doctor.

Warning: Do not take Pain Be Gone with other medicines.

Family Connection—*Understanding Medical History Forms*

1 **READ** part of a family medical history form.

PINE VALLEY MEDICAL CENTER

FAMILY MEDICAL HISTORY

Patient's Name: _Tony McCall_

Date of Birth: _01/03/1987_

Medical Record Number: **684960-4894**

Medical Condition	Yes	No	Relationship
diabetes	✓	○	mother
asthma	✓	○	brother
heart disease	✓	○	father
high blood pressure	✓	○	grandfather
kidney disease	○	✓	
alcohol or drug abuse	○	✓	
vision loss	✓	○	grandmother
hearing loss	○	✓	
depression	○	✓	

2 **CIRCLE** *yes* or *no*.

1. Tony's mother has asthma.   yes   (no)
2. Tony's brother has a medical condition.   yes   no
3. Tony's father has high blood pressure.   yes   no
4. Tony's father has heart disease.   yes   no
5. Tony's grandmother has vision loss.   yes   no
6. Tony's mother has hearing loss.   yes   no
7. Tony's grandmother has depression.   yes   no
8. Someone in Tony's family has an alcohol problem.   yes   no

3 WRITE. Complete the conversation. Use Tony's family medical history form.

Doctor: I'd like to ask you about your family medical history. Do you have any family history of heart disease?

Tony: Yes, my father _____. He had a heart attack last year.

Doctor: What about _____?

Tony: Uhm, yes. My grandfather. He has high blood pressure.

Doctor: Okay. Does anyone in your family have diabetes?

Tony: Yes, my mother _____.

Doctor: Now, is there any asthma in your family?

Tony: Uhm yes, my brother _____.

Doctor: How about depression?

Tony: No, no one _____.

Doctor: Anything else?

Tony: Uhm, let me see. . .yes! My grandmother _____. She can't see very well.

4 REAL-LIFE LESSON. Get medical information about your family. Ask family members about their medical conditions. Complete the chart.

FAMILY MEDICAL HISTORY

Patient's Name: _____

Date of Birth: _____

Medical Condition	Yes	No	Relationship
diabetes	O	O	
asthma	O	O	
heart disease	O	O	
high blood pressure	O	O	
kidney disease	O	O	
alcohol or drug abuse	O	O	
vision loss	O	O	
hearing loss	O	O	
depression	O	O	

Community Connection — *Reading Medicine Labels*

1 MATCH the word and the meaning.

_b_ 1. anxiety   a. a medicine that helps people with anxiety

_____ 2. drowsiness   b. feeling very nervous

_____ 3. herbal medicines   c. conditions that a medication can cause

_____ 4. tranquilizer   d. medicines made from plants

_____ 5. side effects   e. a feeling of being very sleepy

2 READ the medicine labels.

COUGH STOP

Warnings
- Do not use if you are taking a prescription medication for anxiety or depression.
- Ask a doctor if you have: heart disease, high blood pressure, or diabetes.

MAIN STREET PHARMACY
555-606-8561
17 MAIN STREET
ANYTOWN 50505

RX: 1234

DOE HARRY
555 SCOTT STREET
ANYTOWN 50505

TAKE ONE TABLET THREE TIMES A DAY

CALMEX

Warnings
- Do not use if you are pregnant
- May cause drowsiness. Do not use when driving.
- Do not take with alcohol.
- Ask a doctor if you are taking herbal medicines.

NO REFILL(S)
Date Filled: 11/23/2010

3 CIRCLE the correct words.

1. You **can / cannot** use Cough Stop when you take certain medicines.

2. You should talk to a doctor. You want to take Cough Stop, and you **have diabetes / take herbal medicines.**

3. You should talk to a doctor. You take **Calmex / Cough Stop,** and you take herbal medicines.

4. You should not take **Cough Stop / Calmex** when you are driving a car.

5. **Cough Stop / Calmex** has side effects.

6. **Calmex / Cough Stop** can make you sleepy.

4 **WRITE.** Complete the chart with information about the prescription medication, Calmex.

Name of Medication	What SHOULDN'T you do when you take it?	What SHOULDN'T you take with it?	What are the side effects?	Who can't take it?
Calmex				

5 **WHAT ABOUT YOU?** Do you take any medications? Read the label. Are there warnings? List them.

Name of Medication	What SHOULDN'T you do when you take it?	What SHOULDN'T you take with it?	What are the side effects?	Who can't take it?

6 **REAL-LIFE LESSON.** Ask a family member or a friend about prescription medications. Use these questions or your own.

1. Do you take a prescription medication?

2. What can't you do when you take it?

3. What can't you take with it?

4. Are there any side effects?

5. Who can't take it?

Career Connection—*Health Insurance*

1 READ. Marvin sprained his ankle. He went to the doctor. He received this form from his health insurance company.

Superior Health Care, Inc.
P.O. BOX 899
Madison, NJ 07940

Explanation of Benefits

Marvin Matson

Subscriber Name: Marvin Matson
Certificate Number: 456–78–9012

Group Name: RJR
Group Number: 70432

Type of Service	Charges	Amount allowed	Benefit Paid Applied	Amount Due from Patient
Marvin Matson Davis Health Clinic Ajit Roy, MD X–rays	57.00	29.06	29.06	27.94
Pharmacy	70.20	49.14	49.14	21.06
SUMMARY	127.20	78.20	78.20	49.00

For Assistance, please call: 8:00 a.m. – 4:30 p.m. Monday–Friday **1-800-555-6600**

2 MATCH the questions and answers about Activity 1.

_____ 1. Who is the patient?

_____ 2. Who is the doctor?

_____ 3. What is the total cost of the x-rays?

_____ 4. What is the total bill from the pharmacy?

_____ 5. How much of the bill does the insurance company pay?

_____ 6. How much does Marvin need to pay?

a. Ajit Roy, MD

b. $78.20

c. $49.00

d. Marvin Matson

e. $57.00

f. $70.20

3 CIRCLE the answers about the insurance form in Activity 1.

1. Marvin saw Dr. Colleen Murphy.   yes   no

2. Marvin went to get x-rays.   yes   no

3. The insurance company pays $29.06 for the x-rays.   yes   no

4. Marvin needs to pay $29.06 for the x-rays.   yes   no

5. Marvin needs to pay $21.06 for the pharmacy.   yes   no

6. Marvin has a question about the form. He should
   call Davis Health Clinic at 1-800-555-6600.   yes   no

7. Marvin can call at 8:30 A.M. on Thursday.   yes   no

Technology Connection: Finding Information Online

WRITE. You can use the Internet to find information and compare health insurance. Complete the online form.

Insurance Coverage Online

Your Information

ZIP Code: [＿＿＿＿＿＿]   Requested Coverage Date: [/   /]
(mm/dd/yy)

Person

First name: [＿＿＿＿＿＿＿＿＿]   Gender
                                  ◎ ◎   Date of Birth [/   /]
Last name: [＿＿＿＿＿＿＿＿＿]   M   F   (mm/dd/yy)

Tobacco User
  ◎ ◎   Height: [   ] feet [   ] inches   Weight: [   ] pounds
  Yes No

What is this person's occupation? [＿＿＿＿＿＿＿＿＿＿]

Spouse

First name: [＿＿＿＿＿＿＿＿＿]   Gender
                                  ◎ ◎   Date of Birth [/   /]
Last name: [＿＿＿＿＿＿＿＿＿]   M   F   (mm/dd/yy)

Tobacco User
  ◎ ◎   Height: [   ] feet [   ] inches   Weight: [   ] pounds
  Yes No

What is this person's occupation? [＿＿＿＿＿＿＿＿＿＿]

Coverage desired:

◎ Medical   ◎ Dental   ◎ Vision

Email address: [＿＿＿＿＿＿＿＿]

Practice Test

LISTENING: Choose the best response. Then listen to the conversation and choose the correct answer.

1. What's the problem?
   A. I sprained my wrist last week.
   B. That's fine. Thank you.
   C. How may I help you?
   D. My name is Alan Chen.

2. 911. What is the address of the emergency?
   A. 404-555-9078
   B. My name is Alice Woo.
   C. 967 Oak Street.
   D. My son fell and hit his head.

3. What is the problem?
   A. The man sprained his wrist.
   B. The man broke his wrist.
   C. The man cut his wrist.
   D. The man burned his wrist.

4. What does the doctor want to do?
   A. operate on his wrist
   B. put on a bandage
   C. take out stitches
   D. examine his wrist

5. When is the man's appointment?
   A. Tuesday, January 10 at 9:15 A.M.
   B. Tuesday, January 10 at 11:30 A.M.
   C. Wednesday, January 11 at 9:00 A.M.
   D. Wednesday, January 11 at 11:30 A.M.

GRAMMAR AND VOCABULARY: Choose the correct words or phrases to complete each sentence.

6. Sam _____ to work last week.
   A. walk
   B. walks
   C. walked
   D. walking

7. Sara _____ her arm yesterday.
   A. break
   B. broke
   C. breaks
   D. breaking

8. Bob _____ his arm and _____ burn cream last weekend.
   A. burns / applies
   B. burned / applies
   C. burn / apply
   D. burned / applied

9. Jack hurt his wrist, but he didn't _____ it.
   A. sprain
   B. sprained
   C. sprains
   D. spraining

10. Sue went to the library last night. She didn't _____ to the gym.
    A. went
    B. go
    C. goes
    D. going

11. Today is Sunday. I went to the doctor on Friday. I went to the doctor _____.
    A. this morning
    B. four days ago
    C. yesterday
    D. the day before yesterday

12. This year is 2010. Amy joined a gym in 2009. She joined a gym _____ .
   A. last month
   B. yesterday
   C. last week
   D. last year

13. Joe is taking _____ because he has an infection.
   A. cough syrup
   B. insulin
   C. asthma
   D. antibiotics

14. Marie can't eat sugar because she has _____ .
   A. insulin
   B. diabetes
   C. infection
   D. antihistamines

15. Rob cut his finger. He went to the emergency room and got _____ .
   A. stitches
   B. cough syrup
   C. insulin
   D. a cast

16. The doctor put on burn cream. Another word for put on is _____ .
   A. cut
   B. applied
   C. examined
   D. checked

READING: Read the paragraph. Choose the correct answer.

CLEVELAND

Jane Taylor, a 5th Grade student at Pine Valley Elementary School, saved her teacher's life on Friday afternoon. The teacher, Sam Green, and his students ate lunch in the classroom that day. At about 12:15, Mr. Green stopped talking. He couldn't breathe. He had a piece of apple in the back of his throat. Jane put her arm across Green's chest and hit him on the back five times. Green coughed and the piece of apple came out. Green said, "I am so thankful. We just had a first-aid lesson at school last week!"

17. Where did the story happen?
   A. at home
   B. at lunchtime
   C. in the morning
   D. in a classroom

18. What is the best title for the story?
   A. 5th Grade Student Saves Teacher's Life
   B. 5th Grade Teacher Saves Student's Life
   C. 5th Grade Teacher Stops Breathing
   D. 5th Grade Eats Lunch in Classroom

19. Jane put her arm _____ .
   A. around his throat
   B. across his chest
   C. on his back
   D. under his neck

20. Green coughed, and then _____ .
   A. he couldn't breathe
   B. he ate lunch
   C. the piece of apple came out
   D. the class had a first-aid lesson

Lesson 1

1 MATCH the conversation with the picture.

a. *A:* Did the delivery person deliver the package?
   B: Yes, he did.

b. *A:* Did the computer technician help the customer?
   B: Yes, she did.

c. *A:* Did the carpenter build a table?
   B: No, he didn't.

d. *A:* Did she pay the repairperson?
   B: Yes, she did.

e. *A:* Did the stockperson stock the shelves?
   B: Yes, she did.

f. *A:* Did the car mechanics repair the car?
   B: No, they didn't.

Lesson 2

2 **MATCH** the person and the job.

_____ 1. office assistant

_____ 2. plumber

_____ 3. salesclerk

_____ 4. painter

_____ 5. carpenter

_____ 6. delivery person

a. paint the house

b. build a table

c. repair the toilet

d. deliver the boxes

e. help the customer

f. make copies

3 **WRITE** questions about the people and jobs in Activity 2. Use the past tense.

1. _Did the office assistant make copies?_ _____

2. _____

3. _____

4. _____

5. _____

6. _____

4 **WRITE.** Complete the crossword puzzle.

ACROSS

4. another word for *make*

6. This person puts things on shelves.

7. another word for *fix*

DOWN

1. This person makes beds.

2. take things to people

3. This person fixes cars.

5. This person gives change.

6. another way to say *put things on shelves*

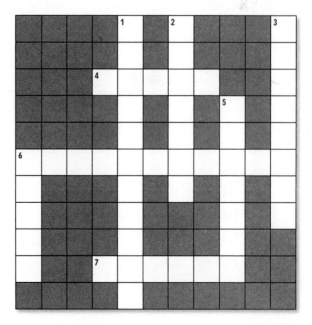

Lesson 3

1 LISTEN. Does the question or answer go up ▲ or down ▼? Circle the correct arrow.

1. (▲)   ▼   6. ▲   ▼
2. ▲   ▼   7. ▲   ▼
3. ▲   ▼   8. ▲   ▼
4. ▲   ▼   9. ▲   ▼
5. ▲   ▼   10. ▲   ▼

2 LISTEN to the question. Then listen to the conversation. Fill in the correct answer.

1. Ⓐ   Ⓑ   Ⓒ
2. Ⓐ   Ⓑ   Ⓒ
3. Ⓐ   Ⓑ   Ⓒ

3 WRITE. Put the lines of the conversation in the correct order. The first one is done for you.

Yes, I did. I ordered them yesterday.

That's okay. You can do it tomorrow. Did you order parts for Dr. Green's computer?

I installed new software on Ms. Park's computer.

What else did you do today?

No, I didn't.

~~Did you repair Dr. Lee's printer?~~

A: _Did you repair Dr. Lee's printer?_____

B: _____

A: _____

_____

B: _____

A: _____

_____

B: _____

_____

Culture and Communication — *Being Positive*

1 **LISTEN** to the conversations. Circle the correct words from the conversations. Then practice the conversations with a partner.

WCD, 34

1
A: Did you **repair** / **install** engines?
B: Yes, I did. I love to **repair** / **install** engines.

2
A: Did you **use** / **repair** computers?
B: No, I didn't, but I **used** / **repaired** other machines.

3
A: Did you **install** / **write** software?
B: No, I didn't, but **I'd like to learn** / **I learn quickly**.

2 **WRITE.** Complete the sentences. Use the phrases in the box or your own ideas.

delivered packages	fixed computers	like to learn
made copies	repaired trucks	was very good

1. I didn't load trucks, but I _____ *delivered packages* _____.

2. I helped customers, and I _____, too.

3. I ordered supplies, and I also _____.

4. I repaired cars, and I also _____.

5. I didn't use computers, but I'd _____.

Useful Expressions
Ways to Be Positive
Yes, I did. I like/love to….
Yes, I did… And I also . . .
Yes, I did. I was very good, too.
No, I didn't, but I ….
No, I didn't, but I'd like to learn.
No, I didn't, but I learn quickly.

3 **WRITE.** Complete the conversation. Then practice the conversation with a partner.

Ms. Chan: Good afternoon. My name is Ms. Chan.

Ken: (1) _____, Ms. Chan. I'm Ken Davis.

Ms. Chan: So, what did you do at your last job, Ken?

Ken: I delivered refrigerators and ovens.

Ms. Chan: Did you repair refrigerators?

Ken: Yes, I (2) _____ refrigerators.

Ms. Chan: Great. Did you install ovens?

Ken: No, but (3) _____.

Lesson 4

1 **MATCH** the questions and the answers.

_d_   1. Why did you leave your last job?   a. I left my last job in April.

_____ 2. Who did you report to on your last job?   b. I graduated in 2008.

_____ 3. What did you do at your last job?   c. I worked at a hospital.

_____ 4. When did you graduate?   d. I left because I moved here.

_____ 5. When did you leave your last job?   e. I installed software.

_____ 6. Where did you work?   f. I reported to the manager.

2 **WRITE.** Unscramble the questions. Then write answers.

1. *A:* last / year / did / work / Where / you / ? _Where did you work last year?_

    B: _I worked at a hotel._

2. *A:* your / job / did / What / do / at / you / last / ? _____

    B: _____

3. *A:* last / did / How / get / work / you / to / week / ? _____

    B: _____

4. *A:* last / Why / you / leave / your / did / job / ? _____

    B: _____

3 **WHAT ABOUT YOU?** Write questions for a friend or family member. Use *How, When, Where, What, Who,* or *Why* and the verbs in the box. Ask the questions. Then write the answers on the lines.

come	do	get	learn

1. *A:* _Where did you learn English?_

    B: _I learned English in elementary school._

2. *A:* _____

    B: _____

3. *A:* _____

    B: _____

4. *A:* _____

    B: _____

Lesson 5

1 **WRITE.** Complete the interview. Use the past tense of the verbs in parentheses.

A: (get) Where _____ you _____ your A.A. degree?

B: (get) I _____ my degree at Pine Valley Community College.

A: (graduate) When _____ you _____?

B: (graduate) I _____ in 2006.

A: (do) What _____ you _____ on your last job?

B: (repair / install) On my last job, I _____ and _____ ovens and refrigerators.

A: (work) Where _____ you _____?

B: (work) I _____ for The Home SuperStore.

A: (report to) Who _____ you _____?

B: (report to) I _____ Ms. Fine, my manager.

A: (leave) Why _____ you _____?

B: (leave) I _____ because my wife got a job in Greenville.

2 **WRITE.** Complete the paragraph with the past tense forms of the verbs in parentheses.

Yesterday, I (1) _____had_____ (have) an interview at Excellent Computer Corporation.

I (2) _____ (prepare) for the interview. I (3) _____ (go) to the company website,

and I (4) _____ (learn) all about the company before the interview. My interview

(5) _____ (be) at 9:00 A.M., and I (6)_____ (be) on time. I (7)_____

(dress) neatly. I (8) _____ (wear) my new black suit. During the interview, I

(9) _____ (ask) questions, and I (10) _____ (make) eye contact.

I (11) _____ (send) a thank-you note after the interview. I think the interview

(12) _____ (go) well!

PAST.

Did you have an interview yesterday
How did you prepare for the interview
What time was your interview
Were you on time for your interview
What did you wear for
Did you ask questions make eye contact.

Rvest Do you think it want well ?

Family Connection—*Matching Job Histories and Job Ads*

1 MATCH the word or phrase and the picture.

_b_ 1. plumbing fixture

_D_ 2. register

_E_ 3. building displays

_C_ 4. making bank deposits

_A_ 5. office equipment

2 READ the job ads.

Trader Dan's Market is looking for part-time cashiers. Must have experience. High school graduate preferred. Duties include using the register, helping customers, building displays, and stocking shelves.
Please apply in person at the store Monday thru Friday 10–4.

The Home SuperStore is looking for plumbers. Must have 2 years experience. Plumbers deliver, repair, and install plumbing fixtures. Must have state license.
Apply online at the company Web site.

Davis Medical Clinic is looking for an office assistant. Duties include: Answering phones, ordering supplies, and making bank deposits. Must know how to use office equipment and office computer programs. If interested, please call 444–555–7968

3 CIRCLE *yes* or *no*.

1. Trader Dan's is looking for an office assistant.	yes	**no**
2. The Home SuperStore is looking for plumbers.	**yes**	no
3. Davis Medical Clinic is looking for a cashier.	yes	**no**
4. You need experience for the office assistant job.	**yes**	no
5. You need a license for the plumber job.	**yes**	no
6. You need to know how to use computers for the cashier's job.	yes	**no**
7. You need experience for the plumber job.	**yes**	no
8. Cashiers at Trader Dan's stock shelves.	**yes**	no

4 **READ** about the people's job histories and answer the questions.

1. Lisa: I graduated from high school last June. During high school, I worked at the dentist's office. I helped patients, I answered phones, and I used a computer.

   What's the best job for Lisa? _She may apply on Davis medical - clinic._

2. Pat: I helped my father build houses. I repaired and installed plumbing fixtures. I want to be a plumber, but I don't have a state license yet.

   Can Pat apply for the job at The Home SuperStore? _No, He can't because He suppose have state license._

3. José: I worked at The Good Food Store for 5 years. I helped customers. I stocked shelves, and I built displays. I didn't use the register, but I learn quickly.

   What job can José probably get? _He can apply on trader Dan's Mar..._

5 **WRITE** sentences about your job history. Use the past forms of verbs. Then answer the question.

I _worked at Landescaping, and maintanence gardens_
I _helped my friend's at siding workers, and Construction_
I _worked at roofing repair, and change at new too. work._
What is a good job for you? _the best job for myself is as a construction worker like as, Remodeling Construction._

6 **REAL-LIFE LESSON.** Ask a family member or friend about his or her job history. Ask questions like these, or ask your own questions. Write the answers in the chart.

Name: _____	
What did you do at your last job?	He set
Where did you work?	
Where did you get your training/ degree/license/certificate?	
Who did you report to?	
Why did you leave your last job?	
What is the best job for you?	

Community Connection—*Having an Information Interview*

1 MATCH the word or term and the meaning.

___*b*___ 1. mentioned

_____ 2. advice

_____ 3. a bachelor's degree

_____ 4. an associate's degree / A.A. degree

a.   a degree from a 4-year college or university

b.   wrote or said

c.   helpful information

d.   a degree from a 2-year college

2 READ the conversation.

Mr. Jackson:	Hi, Gloria. Take a seat.
Gloria:	Hello, Mr. Jackson. Thank you very much for seeing me today.
Mr. Jackson:	It's a pleasure. How can I help you?
Gloria:	As I mentioned in my email, I would like a career as a computer technician. Can you give me some advice? How did you get started?
Mr. Jackson:	Well, I got a computer technician certificate at Pine Valley Community college. Then I went to Greenville State University and got a bachelor's degree in computer engineering.
Gloria:	Do I need a bachelor's degree in computer engineering?
Mr. Jackson:	Not always. We hire technicians with A.A. degrees and certificates here at Excellent Computer Corporation.
Gloria:	How did you find your job?
Mr. Jackson:	I always wanted to work at Excellent Computer Corporation. I found a job ad on the company Web site, and I applied for it. It was a computer technician job. And here I am today, a manager.
Gloria:	Is there anyone else here that you think I should talk to?
Mr. Jackson:	Yes. You should also talk to Mike McCall. His experience is similar to yours. I'll send you his email address.
Gloria:	Well, thank you so much, Mr. Jackson. I really appreciate your help.

3 CIRCLE the correct words.

1. Mr. Jackson is **(happy)** / **unhappy** to help Gloria.

2. Gloria calls the man **Jack** / **Mr. Jackson**.

3. Gloria wants a career as a computer **technician** / **engineer**.

4. Gloria wants **advice** / **a job** from Mr. Jackson.

5. You **do** / **do not** need a bachelor's degree to get a technician job at Excellent Computer Corporation.

6. Mr. Jackson has a **college degree** / **certificate** in computer engineering.

7. Mr. Jackson's first job at Excellent Computer Corporation was a **manager** / **technician** job.

8. Mr. Jackson found a job ad **in a newspaper** / **online**.

9. Gloria wants **advice** / **a job** from another person at the Excellent Computer Corporation.

10. There **is** / **isn't** another person at the Excellent Computer Corporation for Gloria to talk to.

4 WHAT ABOUT YOU? Think of a job and company you like. Write a list of questions for an information interview.

Job title: _____   **Company:** _____

1. _____

2. _____

3. _____

4. _____

5. _____

6. _____

5 REAL-LIFE LESSON. Have an information interview with a family member or a friend. Use these questions or your own.

1. Can you give me some advice?

2. How did you get started?

3. Is it necessary to have a degree/certificate/license?

4. How did you find your job?

5. Is there anyone else that you think I should talk to?

Career Connection—*Writing a Thank-You Letter*

1 READ. Oscar wrote a thank-you letter to Lena. He thanked her for the interview. He told her again things that he said in the interview. He talked about the future. Read Oscar's letter.

> **Oscar Santos**
> 342 Pine Lane
> Granada Hills, CA 91344
>
> Dear Lena,
>
> Thank you very much for giving me the opportunity to have an interview with you. I enjoyed talking with you and learning more about the manager position.
>
> As I mentioned, I think that I would be an excellent manager. I have management experience, and I really enjoy working with people. I'm organized and I'm a hard worker. I like working at the restaurant, and I want it to be successful.
>
> Thank you again. I look forward to hearing from you soon.
>
> Sincerely,
>
> Oscar Santos

2 MATCH the questions and answers about the letter.

_____ 1. How many paragraphs does the letter have?

_____ 2. How many times does Oscar say "thank you"?

_____ 3. Where does Oscar say the name of the job he wants?

_____ 4. Where does Oscar repeat some things he said in the interview?

_____ 5. What does Oscar talk about in the last paragraph?

a. in the 1st paragraph

b. in the 2nd paragraph

c. 3 paragraphs

d. the future

e. 2 times

3 WRITE answers to these questions about the letter.

1. Why did Oscar write the letter? _____

2. What job does Oscar want? _____

3. Why does Oscar want this job? _____

4. What kind of experience does Oscar have? _____

5. What positive things does Oscar say about himself in the letter? _____

_____

4 **READ.** Oscar always checks his spelling when he writes a letter. First, he uses his computer's spell-check program. Then he prints the letter and checks it again. Look at the computer spell-check program.

Spelling and Grammar

Not in dictionary:

wourd

Suggestions:

word
wood
would

Ignore

Change

Cancel

5 **CIRCLE** the correct words.

1. You open **Spelling and Grammar / Suggestions** to start the spell-check program.

2. The spell-check program checks **every word / some words** in your document.

3. The program gives you suggestions when it finds a **wrong / correct** word.

4. You click **Ignore / Change** to correct a mistake.

5. You click **Ignore / Cancel** when you don't want to change a word.

6 **PRACTICE.** Type your answers to Activity 3 on a computer. Use a spell-check program. You can also print your letter and look for mistakes. Change any misspelled words.

Practice Test

LISTENING: Choose the best response. Then listen to the conversation and choose the correct answer.

1. What did you do today?
   A. No, I didn't.
   B. I worked Monday through Friday.
   C. That's O.K.
   D. I painted the living room.

2. Did you deliver the bookcase?
   A. No, I didn't.
   B. That's O.K.
   C. You can do it tomorrow.
   D. No, thank you.

3. Why is Alan talking to Ms. Jones?
   A. to make an appointment for an interview
   B. to interview for a job
   C. to get help with his computer
   D. to learn about installing software

4. What did Alan do on his last job?
   A. He installed software and repaired computers.
   B. He helped customers and delivered computers.
   C. He managed a store.
   D. He repaired computers and helped customers.

5. Why did Alan leave his last job?
   A. He became a store manager.
   B. He got a job in Greenville.
   C. He graduated from college and moved to Greenville.
   D. He started college in Greenville.

GRAMMAR AND VOCABULARY: Choose the correct word or phrase to complete each sentence.

6. _____ you help customers on your last job?
   A. Does
   B. Did
   C. Doing
   D. Do

7. Did the plumber _____ the bathtub?
   A. installs
   B. installed
   C. installing
   D. install

8. A: Did the delivery person deliver the package?
   B: No, she _____ .
   A. didn't
   B. did
   C. don't
   D. does

9. A: Did the carpenter build the shelves?
   B: Yes, he _____ .
   A. doesn't
   B. did
   C. does
   D. do

10. Where did you _____ last year?
    A. works
    B. worked
    C. working
    D. work

11. A: _____ did you graduate?
    B: I graduated last year.
    A. Where
    B. How
    C. When
    D. Why

12. The person you report to is usually _____.
   A. your company
   B. your server
   C. your customer
   D. your boss

13. Office assistants _____.
   A. build bookshelves
   B. make copies
   C. fix cars
   D. help patients

14. Housekeepers _____.
   A. make change
   B. make beds
   C. help patients
   D. prepare food

15. Did the mechanic fix the car yesterday? Another word for fix is _____.
   A. help
   B. repair
   C. deliver
   D. install

16. Did you find out about the job on the Internet? Another way to say *find out* is _____.
   A. lose
   B. learn about
   C. leave
   D. graduate

READING: Read the email. Then answer the questions.

☼ SUNNYMAIL.COM

| Home | Chat | Check mail | Compose | Search mail | Search Web |

(3) Inbox
Draft
(1) Sent
Bulk
Trash

To: tara.white@fmail.com **From:** samchoy@sunnymail.com

Dear Ms. White,

Thank you for talking to me yesterday. I'm glad you can meet me on Wednesday at 1:00 P.M. I have many questions for you about a career as a restaurant manager. Here are a few of my questions.

Where did you get your training?
Do you have a certificate or a college degree?
How did you find your first job?

You asked me about my last job. I worked as an assistant manager at Aqua Bella Restaurant. I served food and ordered supplies. I helped the manager make work schedules for the other employees. I left my last job because I moved to Denver.

I am looking forward to meeting you.

Sincerely,
Sam Choy

17. Who wrote the email?
   A. Ms. White
   B. Aqua Bella
   C. Sam
   D. Tara

18. Why is Sam meeting Ms. White?
   A. for a job interview
   B. for an information interview
   C. to make an appointment
   D. to make a reservation at a restaurant

19. What did Sam not do at his last job?
   A. Manage the restaurant
   B. Order supplies
   C. Serve food
   D. Help make work schedules

20. Why did Sam leave his last job?
   A. He got a job at Aqua Bella Restaurant.
   B. He became the manager.
   C. He moved to Denver.
   D. He moved from Denver.

UNIT 7 Places in My Life

LESSON 1

1 **MATCH** the picture and the sentences. Write the letters in the circles.

a. They were bored.

b. She was excited.

c. They were comfortable.

d. He was uncomfortable.

e. She was calm.

f. He was nervous.

2 **CIRCLE** the correct form of the verb.

1. (Was) / Were Sara in Canada last year?

2. Rob and Nick **was / were** excited about their trip to Mexico.

3. When **were / was** your trip to Spain?

4. How **was / were** your trip to New York?

5. I **wasn't / weren't** comfortable on the plane.

6. My mother **wasn't / weren't** worried about the trip.

7. Where **was / were** Raul and Tom last week?

8. Who **was / were** on the plane with you?

LESSON 2

1 WRITE. Unscramble the sentences.

1. Rob / weren't / during / and Nick / flight / the / uncomfortable / .   _Rob and Nick weren't_
   uncomfortable during the flight.

2. in / When / you / Mexico / were / ? _____

3. uncomfortable / on / was / Sara / plane / the / . _____

4. excited / was / I / trip / about / the / . _____

5. to / was / your / Chicago / trip / How / ? _____

6. New York / Raul / bored / in / wasn't / . _____

2 MATCH the picture and the word.

a. cloudy   c. freezing   e. cool

b. foggy   d. stormy   f. windy

3 WRITE. Complete the paragraph. Use the correct past tense forms of *be* or *be + not*.

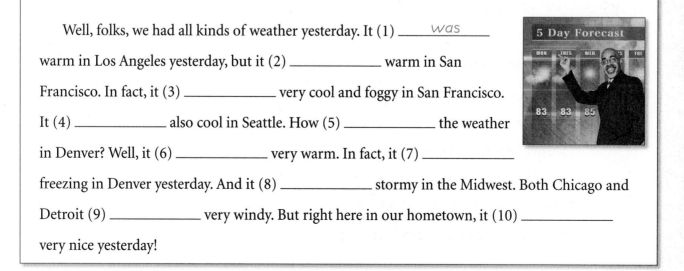

Well, folks, we had all kinds of weather yesterday. It (1) ___was___ warm in Los Angeles yesterday, but it (2) _____ warm in San Francisco. In fact, it (3) _____ very cool and foggy in San Francisco. It (4) _____ also cool in Seattle. How (5) _____ the weather in Denver? Well, it (6) _____ very warm. In fact, it (7) _____ freezing in Denver yesterday. And it (8) _____ stormy in the Midwest. Both Chicago and Detroit (9) _____ very windy. But right here in our hometown, it (10) _____ very nice yesterday!

LESSON 3

1 **LISTEN** for *he*, *she*, or *it*. Circle the word you hear.

1. Was **he** / **she** / **it** nervous?
2. Was **he** / **she** / **it** late?
3. Was **he** / **she** / **it** uncomfortable?
4. Was **he** / **she** / **it** in New York?
5. Was **he** / **she** / **it** cool in Chicago?

6. Where was **he** / **she** / **it** born?
7. Why was **he** / **she** / **it** late?
8. Why was **he** / **she** / **it** worried?
9. Who was **he** / **she** / **it** with?
10. Where was **he** / **she** / **it** foggy?

2 **LISTEN** to the question. Then listen to the conversation. Fill in the correct answer.

1. Ⓐ Ⓑ Ⓒ
2. Ⓐ Ⓑ Ⓒ
3. Ⓐ Ⓑ Ⓒ

3 **WRITE.** Complete the conversation with the sentences in the box.

I was nervous.	I came by car.
It was long.	I came here when I was 21 years old.
My brother was with me.	

A: How old were you when you first came to New York?

B: _I came here when I was 21 years old._

A: How did you feel about coming here?

B: _____

A: How did you get here?

B: _____

A: How was your trip?

B: _____

A: Who was with you on your trip?

B: _____

Culture and Communication—*Talking About the Weather*

WCD, 38

1 **LISTEN** to and read the conversation. Then practice it with a partner.

> *Ann:* Hi, Raul.
>
> *Raul:* Hi, Ann. How are you?
>
> *Ann:* Fine. And you?
>
> *Raul:* Okay.
>
> *Ann:* Hey, what about this weather?
>
> *Raul:* Yeah. It's really freezing today!
>
> *Ann:* You're right. And it's windy, too. It's terrible today!

2 **WRITE.** Complete the conversations with expressions from the box.

1. *A:* How about this weather?

   B: I _____!

2. *A:* What about this weather?

   B: It's really _____ today.

   A: You're right. And it's _____ , too.

3 **WRITE** a conversation about the weather today. Then practice your conversation with a partner.

_____

_____

_____

_____

_____

_____

_____

_____

_____

Useful Expressions:
Talking About the Weather
How about this weather?
What about this weather?
What about this weather we're having?
Crazy weather, huh?
I love this weather!
I hate this weather!
It's really hot/cold/freezing/rainy today.
It's nice (weather) today.
It's terrible (weather) today.
It's great (weather) today!

LESSON 4

1 WRITE. Complete the sentences with the comparative form of the adjective in parentheses.

1. My old apartment was big, but my new apartment is _____*bigger*_____ (big).

2. Rob is 21. Nick is 22. Nick is _____ (old) than Rob.

3. Salaries in San Francisco are _____ (good) than salaries in Portland.

4. Apartment rents in New York are _____ (high) than rents in Seattle.

5. Sam has a little work today. Sara has a lot of work today. Sara is _____ (busy) than Sam.

6. The weather in Pittsburgh is bad today. It's _____ (bad) than the weather in New York.

7. San Francisco is _____ (relax) than New York.

8. Chicago and Los Angeles are _____ (noisy) than my city.

2 WRITE. Change each adjective in the chart to a comparative adjective.

San Diego	
sunny	*sunnier*
crowded	
expensive	
big	

Portland	
quiet	
cool	
rainy	
small	

3 WRITE. Use the information in the chart to compare San Diego and Portland. Use *than* in your sentences.

1. *San Diego is sunnier than Portland.*

2. _____

3. _____

4. _____

5. _____

6. _____

7. _____

8. _____

LESSON 5

1 **LISTEN** and complete the chart below.

WCD, 39

	Greenville	**Brownville**
Average salary for workers	$_____ per year	$25,000 per year
Average salary for professionals	$_____ per year	$80,000 per year
Average rent	$800 a month	$_____ a month
Average price of 1 week's groceries	$_____	$200
Population	_____	85,000

professionals—people with careers that require a lot of education and training, like doctors

2 **WRITE.** Complete the sentences with information from the chart. Use the comparative forms of the adjectives below.

big	high	low	small

1. Workers' salaries are _____*higher*_____ in Brownville.

2. The average salary for professionals in Greenville is _____ than the average salary in Brownville.

3. Brownville has a _____ population than Greenville.

4. The population is _____ in Greenville than in Brownville.

5. The price of groceries is _____ in Brownville than in Greenville.

6. Rents are _____ in Greenville than in Brownville.

3 **LISTEN AND CIRCLE** the number you hear.

WCD, 40

1. 4,567   40,567   400,567

2. 6,362   60,362   600,362

3. 2,589   20,589   200,589

4. 7,453   70,453   700,453

5. 1,900   10,900   100,900

6. 3,378   30,378   300,368

7. 34,568   340,568   3,405,680

8. 57,920   579,203   57,920,300

Family Connection—*Interpreting Temperatures in Celsius and Fahrenheit*

1 MATCH the word and the picture.

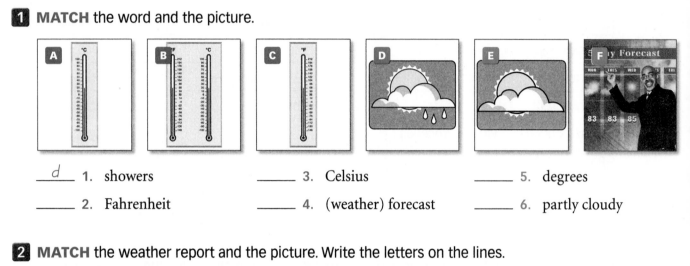

__d__ 1. showers   _____ 3. Celsius   _____ 5. degrees

_____ 2. Fahrenheit   _____ 4. (weather) forecast   _____ 6. partly cloudy

2 MATCH the weather report and the picture. Write the letters on the lines.

_____ 1. Madrid, A Few Showers
66°F (19°C)

_____ 2. Melbourne, Partly Cloudy
60°F (16°C)

_____ 3. Miami, Sunny
81°F (27°C)

_____ 4. Moscow, Snow
32°F (0°C)

3 MATCH the Celsius temperature and the Fahrenheit temperature.

°F	°C	Celsius		Fahrenheit
212	100	__e__ 1. 20°		a. 32°
194	90			
176	80	_____ 2. 4°		b. 60°
158	70			
140	60	_____ 3. 27°		c. 39°
122	50			
104	40	_____ 4. 8°		d. 80°
86	30			
68	20	_____ 5. 16°		e. 68°
50	10			
32	0	_____ 6. 0°		f. 46°
14	-10			
-4	-20			
-22	-30			
-40	-40			
-58	-50			
-76	-60			
-94	-70			
-112	-80			
-130	-90			
-148	-100			

WCD, 41

4 **LISTEN AND WRITE** the temperatures you hear.

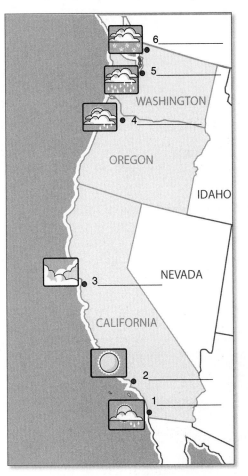

 WCD, 42

5 **LISTEN AND MATCH** the city and the weather word or phrase.

___a___ 1. San Diego   a. warm and partly sunny

_____ 2. Los Angeles   b. cool and very rainy

_____ 3. San Francisco   c. foggy

_____ 4. Portland   d. freezing with snow and ice

_____ 5. Seattle   e. showers

_____ 6. Bellingham   f. warm and sunny

6 **REAL-LIFE LESSON.** Listen to a weather report. Write down the temperatures you hear. Then write sentences about the weather. Use the words in the box or your own words.

cloudy	cool	foggy	freezing	ice	nice	partly cloudy
rainy	showers	snow	sunny	terrible	warm	

_____

_____

Community Connection—*Understanding a Five-Day Forecast*

1 READ about Teresa.

_b_ 1. humidity   a. a camera that shows pictures on the web

___ 2. current   b. moisture (water) in the air

___ 3. overcast   c. North, South, East, West

___ 4. web cam   d. cloudy

___ 5. °   e. right now

___ 6. N, S, E, W   f. miles per hour

___ 7. mph   g. "degree" or "degrees"

2 READ a weather forecast on a web page.

```
www.weathertoday.com
```

FIND YOUR LOCAL WEATHER FORECAST   [enter zip code, or city] [GO]   maps photos video alerts

| yesterday | today | tomorrow | hour by hour | five day | month |

**Right now in Seattle, WA
Current Conditions**

58°F

Overcast
Wind: N 5 mph
Humidity: 81%

Web Cam
Live in Seattle

[play]
[stop]

Today	Wednesday	Thursday	Friday	Saturday
High/Low °F	High/Low °F	High/Low °F	High/Low °F	High/Low °F
77/57	79/55	77/56	73/56	65/57

3 CIRCLE the correct words.

1. Right now, it's **sunny / cloudy** in Seattle.

2. The wind is coming from the **north / south**.

3. The wind is **50 / 5** miles per hour.

4. The humidity is **81% / 58%**.

5. Today is **Tuesday / Wednesday**.

6. The low temperature today is **77 / 57**.

7. The high temperature on Saturday is **65 / 57**.

8. The weather is getting **cloudier / sunnier** this week.

4 **WRITE** sentences about last week's weather in Seattle. Use the comparative forms of the adjectives in parentheses. Use past tense forms of *be*.

1. (high) temperature / Wednesday / Tuesday.

   The temperature on Wednesday was higher than the temperature on Tuesday. .

2. (cloudy) it / on Tuesday / Wednesday.

   _____ .

3. (sunny) it/ Friday / Saturday.

   _____ .

4. (cool) it / Saturday / Friday.

   _____ .

5. (warm) weather / Wednesday / Thursday.

   _____ .

5 **REAL-LIFE LESSON.** Find a five-day forecast on the web or in the newspaper. Complete the chart. Include Fahrenheit temperatures and weather words for each day.

Five-Day Forecast for (place):				
Today	_____	_____	_____	_____
High/Low °F	High/Low °F	High/Low °F	High/Low °F	High/Low °F

Career Connection—*Learning About a New Place Before You Move*

1 READ. Sofia got a new job and moved to a new city. Before she moved, she learned all about the new city on the web.

---

www.chamberofcommerce.com

CHAMBER OF COMMERCE   search our site GO

Home
Consumer Topics
General Buying Tips
Shopping From Home
Protect Your Identity
Protect Your Privacy
Automobiles
Banking
Credit
Education
Employment
Food and Nutrition
Health Care
Housing
Insurance
Investing
Relocation
Travel
Utilities

Business Topics
Links
About US
Resource Directory

A Great Place to Live!
Green City, OH
Population: 52,900

Financial

Average family income:	$50,836
Average auto insurance (per year):	$1,485

Housing

Average home price:	$106,935
Average apartment rent: (one-bedroom)	$500

Weather

Annual rainfall (inches):	40
Percent of clear days:	21
High temperature in July °F:	86°
Low temperature in January °F:	18°

---

2 MATCH the questions and answers.

_____ 1. What is the population of Green City?   a. $500

_____ 2. What is the average family income in Green City?   b. 40

_____ 3. What is the average rent for a one-bedroom apartment? c. 86°

_____ 4. How many inches of rainfall are there each year?   d. 52,900

_____ 5. What is the high temperature in July?   e. $50,836

_____ 6. What is the low temperature in January?   f. 18°

3 WRITE. Compare Green City with your town. Write sentences.

1. _____

2. _____

3. _____

4. _____

5. _____

Sofia used an online map to get directions from her new apartment to her job.

A **READ** the directions from an online mapping program.

⊗ ⊖ ⊕   www.map-it-out.com

MAP-IT-OUT

| Turn by Turn | Map | start: | finish: | GO |

PRINT   EMAIL   REVERSE   CHANGE ROUTE

Directions
Total est. Time: 12 minutes
Total est. Distance: 6.62 miles   Distance

START	1:	Start out going NORTH on Pine Road toward Oak Street.	0.1 miles
➡	2:	Turn RIGHT onto Oak Street.	1.2 miles
⬆	3:	Oak Street becomes Valley Blvd.	4.5 miles
⬅	4:	Turn LEFT onto Green Street.	0.3 miles
➡	5:	Turn RIGHT onto Cherry Street.	0.2 miles
➡	6:	Turn RIGHT onto Main Street.	0.1 miles
FINISH	7:	End at 5678 Main Street.	

B **CIRCLE** the correct words and numbers.

1. You start out going **south** / **north** on Pine Road.

2. You turn **right** / **left** onto Oak Street.

3. You drive for **1.2** / **0.1** miles on Oak Street.

4. You **go straight on** / **turn right onto** Valley Blvd.

5. You turn **left** / **right** onto Main Street.

6. The total distance is **1.2** / **6.62** miles.

7. The total estimated time is **12** / **20** minutes.

8. The address is **5876** / **5678** Main Street.

Practice Test

LISTENING: Choose the best response. Then listen to the conversation and choose the correct answer.

1. How old were you when you came to this city?
   - A. I was nervous.
   - B. I was exciting.
   - C. I came by bus.
   - D. I was 14.

2. How did you get here?
   - A. I was afraid.
   - B. I came by train.
   - C. I was short.
   - D. I was 17.

3. When did Alan come here?
   - A. when he was 6
   - B. when he was 7
   - C. when he was 11
   - D. when he was 17

4. How did Alan get here?
   - A. by train
   - B. by car
   - C. by bus
   - D. by plane

5. How was his trip?
   - A. slow
   - B. long
   - C. short
   - D. fast

GRAMMAR AND VOCABULARY: Choose the correct word or phrase to complete each sentence.

6. Anna _____ uncomfortable on the trip.
   - A. were
   - B. was
   - C. be
   - D. who

7. _____ Rob and Nick late again?
   - A. Who
   - B. Where
   - C. Were
   - D. Was

8. It _____ foggy in San Francisco.
   - A. were
   - B. was
   - C. where
   - D. be

9. They were comfortable on the trip. They _____ uncomfortable.
   - A. were
   - B. was
   - C. wasn't
   - D. weren't

10. _____ you late?
    - A. Why were
    - B. Why was
    - C. Why wasn't
    - D. Who was

11. _____ your trip?
    - A. Who were
    - B. How was
    - C. When were

12. Portland is _____ Los Angeles.
    A. rain
    B. rainy
    C. rainier than
    D. rainier

13. Anna is _____ Amy.
    A. more worried than
    B. worried
    C. worried than
    D. worry that

14. The opposite of *calm* is _____.
    A. nervous
    B. comfortable
    C. relaxed
    D. warm

15. The number of people living in a place is the _____.
    A. life expectancy
    B. salary
    C. population
    D. cost

16. Another word for *relaxed* is _____.
    A. stressful
    B. nervous
    C. calm
    D. bored

READING: Read the letter. Choose the correct answer.

Dear Sam,

Thanks for your letter. It was nice to hear from you. You asked how I am doing.

I'm very happy. San Francisco is different from my hometown. The streets in San Francisco are more crowded. The supermarkets are bigger, but I think the food in my hometown was better. The weather was better in my hometown, but it was colder. In some ways, my new town is similar to my hometown. Both towns are near the ocean, and I really like that.

Well, that's all for now. Write again soon.

Your friend,
Rob

17. Who wrote the letter?
    A. Rob's friend
    B. Sam
    C. Sam's brother
    D. Rob

18. What is the main idea of the letter?
    A. San Francisco is more crowded than Rob's hometown.
    B. San Francisco is different from and similar to Rob's hometown.
    C. San Francisco is very different from Rob's hometown.
    D. San Francisco is near the ocean.

19. Supermarkets are _____.
    A. bigger in San Francisco
    B. better in San Francisco
    C. the same in both places
    D. more crowded in San Francisco

20. Both places _____.
    A. are cold
    B. have good food
    C. are near the ocean
    D. have good weather

UNIT **8** **Food and Nutrition**

Lesson 1

1 **MATCH** the picture and the word.

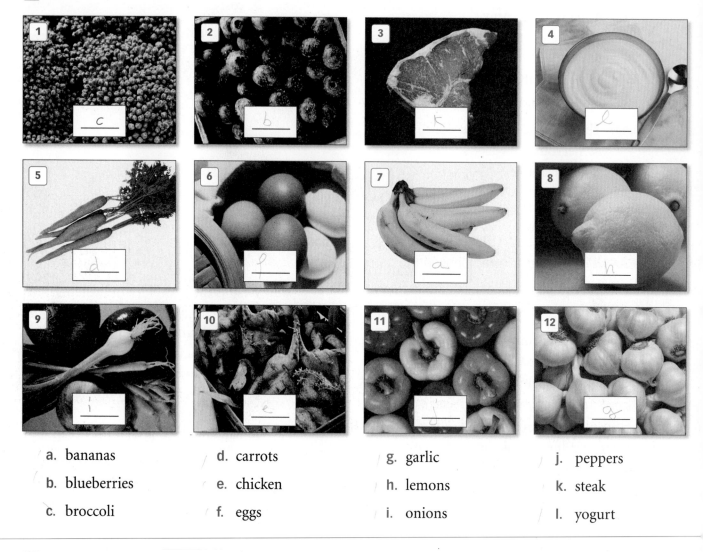

1 _c_	2 _b_	3 _k_	4 _l_
5 _d_	6 _f_	7 _a_	8 _h_
9 _i_	10 _e_	11 _j_	12 _g_

a. bananas
b. blueberries
c. broccoli

d. carrots
e. chicken
f. eggs

g. garlic
h. lemons
i. onions

j. peppers
k. steak
l. yogurt

2 **WRITE** a quantifier for each food word in Activity 1. Use the words and phrases in the box. You can use more than one quantifier for some items.

a	an	a couple of	a few	a little bit of	a lot of	one	several	some

1. _____some_____ bananas

2. _____ steak

3. _____ carrots

4. _____ broccoli

5. _____ onions

6. _____ peppers

7. _____ blueberries

8. _____ yogurt

9. _____ eggs

10. _____ lemons

11. _____ chicken

12. _____ garlic

Lesson 2

1 CIRCLE the correct container.

1. We need two **(cans)/ boxes** of tuna.
2. Can you buy a **bag / loaf** of bread?
3. Sam bought two **bunches / boxes** of grapes today.
4. I had a **box / bag** of chips for lunch.

5. We have one **jar / bag** of mustard.
6. Luis has two **cartons / jars** of juice.
7. We need a **box / bunch** of bananas.
8. Marta needs one **can / bottle** of soup.

2 WRITE. Do the math. Complete the chart. Then circle the juice that has the best price.

Item	Total Price	Total Number of Quarts	Price per quart Total price ÷ Total # of quarts
Juice A	$6.00	4	$ _6.00_ ÷ _4_ = $ _1.50_
Juice B	$3.40	2	$ ___ ÷ ___ = $ _1.70_
Juice C	$1.60	1	$ ___ ÷ ___ = $ _1.60_

3 WRITE. Complete the paragraph about the picture. Use the quantifiers in Lesson 1, Activity 2. You can use more than one quantifier for some items.

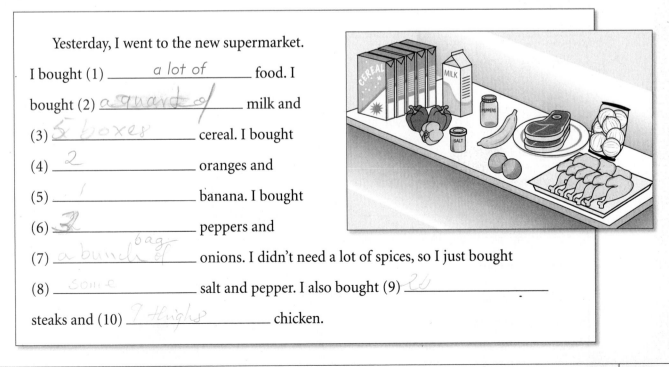

Yesterday, I went to the new supermarket.
I bought (1) ___a lot of___ food. I
bought (2) _a quart of_ milk and
(3) _5 boxes_ cereal. I bought
(4) _2_ oranges and
(5) _1_ banana. I bought
(6) _3_ peppers and
(7) _a bunch of / bag_ onions. I didn't need a lot of spices, so I just bought
(8) _some_ salt and pepper. I also bought (9) _2_
steaks and (10) _7 thighs_ chicken.

Lesson 3

1 LISTEN. Circle the word you hear.

1. **I like / I'd like** steak.
2. **They like / They'd** like yogurt.
3. **I like / I'd like** milk.
4. **We like / We'd like** eggs.
5. **They like / They'd like** chicken.

6. **I like / I'd like** coffee.
7. **We like / We'd like** peppers.
8. **They like / They'd like** rice.
9. **I like / I'd like** tea.
10. **They like / They'd like** chicken.

2 LISTEN to the conversation. Circle the items that Raul orders.

Liza's

Soups and Salads			Sides	
Onion Soup	cup 4.00	bowl 6.50	French Fries	4.75
Vegetable Soup	cup 4.25	bowl 7.00	Mixed Vegetables	3.25
Chicken Soup	cup 5.00	bowl 7.50	Broccoli	2.50
Green Salad		4.50		
Sandwiches			**Desserts**	
Chicken Sandwich		6.75	Chocolate Cake	4.50
Tuna Sandwich		9.75	Ice Cream (Chocolate or Vanilla)	3.50
Steak Sandwich		12.00	Fruit Bowl	3.00
Hamburger		7.50	**Beverages**	
Cheeseburger		7.75	Iced Tea	1.50
Rice Dishes			Soda (Cola, Lemon–Lime, Orange)	1.70
Rice with Vegetables		8.50	Tea	2.00
Rice with Chicken		9.50	Coffee	2.50
Rice with Beef		10.50	Milk	2.25

3 WRITE. Complete the conversation. Choose items that you want. Use the menu in Activity 2. Then practice the conversation with a partner.

> A: Are you ready to order?
>
> B: Yes, I am.
>
> A: Would you like to start with some soup or salad?
>
> B: Yes. I'd like _____.
>
> A: What would you like for your main course?
>
> B: I'll have _____.
>
> A: Okay. Would you like something to drink?
>
> B: Yes. I'd like _____, please.
>
> A: And would you like something for dessert?
>
> B: Yes, I'll have _____.

Culture and Communication—*Offering, Accepting, and Refusing Food*

1 LISTEN to and read the conversation. Then practice it with a partner.

> *Pedro:* Would you like a little more chicken, Lucia?
>
> *Lucia:* No, thanks, Pedro.
>
> *Pedro:* How about some more rice?
>
> *Lucia:* Yes, please.

Useful Expressions

Ways to Offer

some more
a little more
a/an/another
another } Would you like <u>more</u>?

Can I get you
How about } more/some more/a little more/a/an/another?
Do you want

Would you like anything to drink/eat?
What would you like?
What can I get you?

Polite Ways to Refuse Food

No, thank you. / No, thanks.
Nothing for me, thank you.
That was wonderful, but I just can't eat/drink any more.

Polite Ways to Accept Food

Yes, please. / Yes, thanks.
Yes, thank you.
Just a little more, please.

2 WRITE. Complete the conversations.

1. *A:* _____ some fish?

   B: Yes, _____.

2. *A:* _____ some more potatoes?

   B: No, _____.

3. *A:* _____ some more salad?

   A: Yes, _____.

4. *A:* Can I _____ you something to drink?

   B: Yes, _____. I'll have some coffee.

Lesson 4

1 CIRCLE. Look at the words and abbreviations in the box. Circle the same words and the abbreviations on the yogurt label.

| calcium | calories | g (grams) | iron | protein |

2 READ the questions and answers about the yogurt label. Circle the correct words.

1. *A:* How **much** / **many** servings are in this yogurt container?

   B: There **is** / **are** one serving.

2. *A:* How **much** / **many** ingredients are there?

   B: There aren't **much** / **many** ingredients.

3. *A:* How **much** / **many** calories does a serving have?

   B: One serving doesn't have **much** / **many** calories.

4. *A:* How **much** / **many** protein is there in this yogurt?

   B: There's **many** / **a lot of** protein in it.

5. *A:* Does it have **any** / **many** iron?

   B: Yes, there's **some** / **any** iron.

6. *A:* Is there **any** / **many** calcium?

   B: Yes, there's **many** / **some** calcium.

Nutrition Facts

Serving Size: 1 container (245g)

Ingredients: milk, sugar, natural flavor, pectin, live active cultures.

Amount Per Serving

Calories 160	Calories from Fat 27
	% Daily Value*
Total Fat 3g	5%
Saturated Fat 2g	10%
Trans Fat	
Cholesterol 12mg	4%
Sodium 162mg	7%
Total Carbohydrate 34g	11%
Dietary Fiber 0g	0%
Sugars 34g	
Protein 12g	

| Vitamin A 2% | • | Vitamin C 3% |
| Calcium 42% | • | Iron 1% |

*Percent Daily Values are based on a 2,000 calorie diet. Your daily values may be higher or lower depending on your calorie needs.

NutritionData.com

---

3 WRITE. Unscramble the questions.

1. chicken / much / Is / in / protein / there / ? _Is there much protein in chicken?_

   _____

2. a / of / Are / in / there / ice cream / calories / lot / ? _____

   _____

3. does / have / many / How / calories / apple / an / ? _____

   _____

4. any / Do / protein / have / apples / ? _____

   _____

5. have / much / Does / iron / broccoli / ? _____

   _____

Lesson 5

1 **READ** the cereal labels and complete the chart.

A **Nutrition Facts**
Serving Size: 1 cup (46g)

Amount Per Serving

Calories 170   Calories from Fat 19

	% Daily Value*
Total Fat 2g	3%
Saturated Fat 0g	2%
Trans Fat	
Cholesterol 0mg	0%
Sodium 246mg	10%
Total Carbohydrate 35g	12%
Dietary Fiber 3g	12%
Sugars 16g	
Protein 4g	

Ingredients: oats, sugar, salt, cinnamon, and other spices.

*Percent Daily Values are based on a 2,000 calorie diet. Your daily values may be higher or lower depending on your calorie needs.

NutritionData.com

B **Nutrition Facts**
Serving Size: 1 cup (46g)

Amount Per Serving

Calories 150   Calories from Fat 43

	% Daily Value*
Total Fat 2g	8%
Saturated Fat 1g	4%
Trans Fat	
Cholesterol 0mg	0%
Sodium 3mg	0%
Total Carbohydrate 54g	18%
Dietary Fiber 8g	32%
Sugars 1g	
Protein 13g	

Ingredients: oats, sugar, salt, cinnamon, and other spices.

*Percent Daily Values are based on a 2,000 calorie diet. Your daily values may be higher or lower depending on your calorie needs.

NutritionData.com

	Cereal A	Cereal B
fat	*2g (grams)*	
calories		
sodium		
sugars		*1g (gram)*
protein		

2 **WRITE.** Ask and answer questions about the two nutrition labels. Then answer the questions.

1. (fat) _How much fat does_ Cereal A have? _2 grams_ Cereal B? _2 grams_

2. (calories) _____ Cereal A have? _____ Cereal B? _____

3. (sodium) _____ Cereal A have? _____ Cereal B? _____

4. (sugar) _____ Cereal A have? _____ Cereal B? _____

5. (protein) _____ Cereal A have? _____ Cereal B? _____

Which cereal is better for you? _____

Why? _____

Family Connection—*Understanding Weights and Measures*

1 **MATCH** the measurement and the abbreviation.

___f___ 1. gallon   _____ 5. cup   a. c.   e. tsp.

_____ 2. quart   _____ 6. pint   b. oz.   f. gal.

_____ 3. pound   _____ 7. tablespoon   c. tbs.   g. lb.

_____ 4. ounce   _____ 8. teaspoon   d. qt.   h. pt.

2 **MATCH** the picture and the sentence.

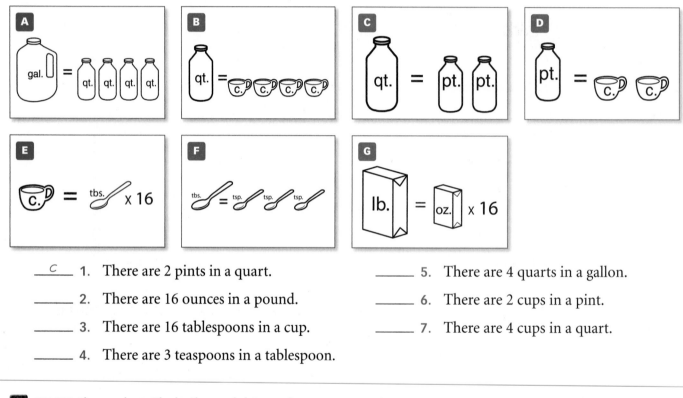

___c___ 1. There are 2 pints in a quart.

_____ 2. There are 16 ounces in a pound.

_____ 3. There are 16 tablespoons in a cup.

_____ 4. There are 3 teaspoons in a tablespoon.

_____ 5. There are 4 quarts in a gallon.

_____ 6. There are 2 cups in a pint.

_____ 7. There are 4 cups in a quart.

3 **READ** the recipe. Circle the weights and measurements.

Cheesy Rice (8 servings)

Ingredients	
3 tbs. olive oil	1 c. chopped tomatoes
1 c. chopped onion	1 tsp. dried basil
2 tbs. chopped garlic	1 tsp. dried oregano
2 c. rice	1 tsp. dried parsley
2 qt. chicken broth (boiling)	8 oz. grated cheese
	salt and pepper

Steps
1. First, put the olive oil in a 4-qt. pot. Heat on medium-high. When the oil is hot, add the chopped onions and garlic. Cook until the onions and garlic are soft.
2. Next, add the rice. Cook it until it becomes a golden color.
3. Then slowly add the boiling chicken broth. Stir the rice. Turn the heat down to low. Let the rice cook for 20 minutes.
4. Finally, add the chopped tomatoes, the dried herbs, and the grated cheese. Stir the rice. Taste it Add a little salt and pepper, if necessary.

4 CIRCLE the correct word.

1. The recipe is for **4 /⑧** people.

2. Two quarts of chicken broth equal **4 / 8** cups.

3. Parsley is a kind of **herb / cheese**.

4. There is a total of **1 / 3** teaspoons of dried herbs in this recipe.

5. Eight ounces of cheese is the same as **1 / $\frac{1}{2}$** pound of cheese.

6. A 4-quart pot is the same as a **1 / 4** gallon pot.

5 WRITE. You have a small family. Rewrite the recipe in Activity 3 for 4 people.

Cheesy Rice (4 servings)

Ingredients

_____ olive oil

_____ chopped onion

_____ chopped garlic

_____ rice

_____ chicken broth (boiling)

_____ chopped tomatoes

_____ dried basil

_____ dried oregano

_____ dried parsley

_____ grated cheese

salt and pepper

Steps

1. First, put the olive oil in a _____ -qt. pot.

6 REAL-LIFE LESSON. Ask a family member or a friend for a recipe. Write the ingredients and instructions below.

Name _____ _____ servings

Ingredients

_____   _____
_____   _____
_____   _____
_____   _____

Steps

1. _____
2. _____
3. _____
4. _____
5. _____

Community Connection—*Understanding Unit Pricing*

1 **MATCH** the word and the meaning.

_____ 1. item price   a. the price of a unit of measure, such as an ounce

_____ 2. a deal   b. something that is good to buy

_____ 3. unit pricing   c. the price of a box, can, a package of food

2 **READ** the unit price labels.

A: CEREAL   12 oz.
Item Price: **$3.92**
Unit Price: **$.32** per oz.

B: CEREAL   18 oz.
Item Price: **$3.79**
Unit Price: **$.21** per oz.

A: MUSHROOM SOUP   16 oz.
Item Price: **$1.44**
Unit Price: **$.09** per oz.

B: MUSHROOM SOUP   19 oz.
Item price: **$1.71**
Unit price: **$.09** per oz.

3 **MATCH** the question and the answer. One answer matches two questions.

_____ 1. Which cereal is smaller?   a. Cereal B

_____ 2. Which cereal has the lower price?   b. Cereal A

_____ 3. What is the unit price of Cereal A?   c. Mushroom Soup A

_____ 4. What is the unit price of Cereal B?   d. $.32

_____ 5. Which mushroom soup is larger?   e. $.09

_____ 6. Which mushroom soup has the lower price?   f. Mushroom Soup B

_____ 7. What is the unit price of Mushroom Soup A?   g. $.21

_____ 8. What is the unit price of Mushroom Soup B?

4 WRITE answers to the questions about the two cereals and two soups.

1. What are three differences between Cereal A and Cereal B? _____

_____

2. Which cereal is a better deal? _____

Why? _____

3. What are two differences between Mushroom Soup A and Mushroom Soup B?

_____

4. Which mushroom soup is a better deal? _____

Why? _____

5 READ about the people. Choose the best deal for each person.

1. Ana wants to save money. Which cereal is best for her? _____

Why? _____

2. Tim lives alone, and he doesn't want to buy a lot of cereal. Which cereal is best for him?

_____

3. Sam has a big family. They like mushroom soup. Which soup is best for him? _____

Why? _____

4. Rob wants some cereal and some soup. He lives alone, and he is going on a long trip in a few days.

Which soup and cereal are best for him? _____

Why? _____

6 REAL-LIFE LESSON. Go to a grocery store. Find two brands of mushroom soup. Read the unit pricing labels. Decide: Which one is the better deal?

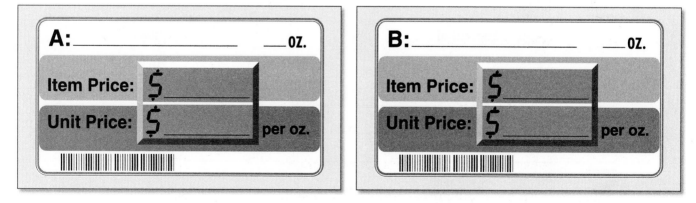

A: _____ ___ OZ.

Item Price: $ _____

Unit Price: $ _____ per oz.

B: _____ ___ OZ.

Item Price: $ _____

Unit Price: $ _____ per oz.

Career Connection—*Eating Healthier Food*

1 READ. Oscar wants to learn about healthy food choices. He found an article on the web. Read the article.

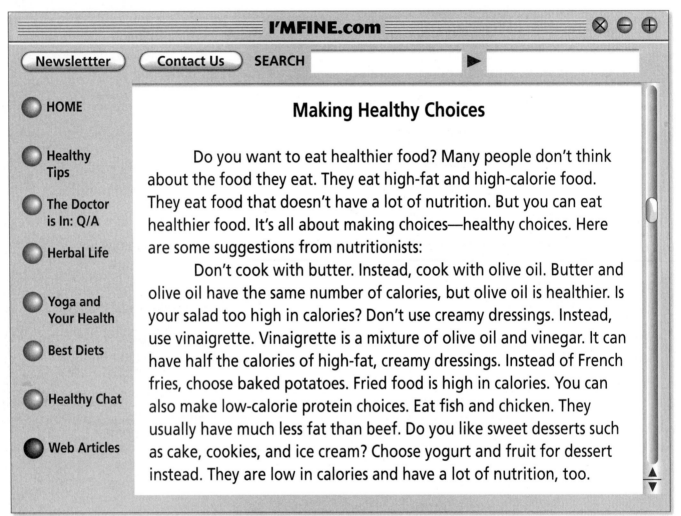

I'MFINE.com

| Newslettter | Contact Us | SEARCH |

- HOME
- Healthy Tips
- The Doctor is In: Q/A
- Herbal Life
- Yoga and Your Health
- Best Diets
- Healthy Chat
- Web Articles

Making Healthy Choices

Do you want to eat healthier food? Many people don't think about the food they eat. They eat high-fat and high-calorie food. They eat food that doesn't have a lot of nutrition. But you can eat healthier food. It's all about making choices—healthy choices. Here are some suggestions from nutritionists:

Don't cook with butter. Instead, cook with olive oil. Butter and olive oil have the same number of calories, but olive oil is healthier. Is your salad too high in calories? Don't use creamy dressings. Instead, use vinaigrette. Vinaigrette is a mixture of olive oil and vinegar. It can have half the calories of high-fat, creamy dressings. Instead of French fries, choose baked potatoes. Fried food is high in calories. You can also make low-calorie protein choices. Eat fish and chicken. They usually have much less fat than beef. Do you like sweet desserts such as cake, cookies, and ice cream? Choose yogurt and fruit for dessert instead. They are low in calories and have a lot of nutrition, too.

2 WRITE. Complete the chart with items from the article.

Instead of . . .	Choose . . .
butter	*olive oil*

3 WHAT ABOUT YOU? What do you think? Add more healthy choices to the chart.

Technology Connection: Getting Nutrition Information Online

Oscar found a website with nutrition information. It gives the calories and nutrition information for hundreds of different food items.

LOOK AND WRITE. Put the steps in order for a nutrition search.

	I'MFINE.com	⊗ ⊖ ⊕

Newslettter   **Contact Us**   SEARCH   Nutrition Information

- HOME
- Healthy Tips
- The Doctor is In: Q/A
- Herbal Life
- Yoga and Your Health
- Best Diets
- Healthy Chat
- Web Articles

Nutrition Information

Keyword Search: ▶

Select Food Group: ▶

SUBMIT

All Food Groups
Baby Foods
Baked Products
Beef Products
Beverages
✓ Breakfast Cereals
Cereal Grains & Pasta
Dairy & Egg Products
Fast Foods
Fats & Oils
Fish and Shellfish Products
Fruits & Fruit Juices
Lamb, Veal, & Game Products
Legumes & Legume Products
Meals, Entrees, & Sidedishes
Nut and Seed Products
Pork Products
Poultry Products
Sausages & Luncheon Meats

_____ Click the submit button.

_____ Select the group the food is in.

_____ Write the name of the food in the Keyword textbox.

4 PRACTICE. You want to find nutrition information for the following foods. Look at the keyword in column 1. Then circle the correct name of the food group in column 2.

Keyword	Food Group
canned tuna	(Fish and Shellfish) / Sweets
olive oil	Fats & Oils / Snacks
orange juice	Dairy and Egg Products / Fruits and Fruit Juices
potato chips	Snacks / Soups, Sauces, & Gravies
bananas	Fast Foods / Fruits and Fruit Juices
ground beef	Beef Products / Fish and Shellfish

Practice Test

WCD, 47

LISTENING: Choose the best response. Then listen to the conversation and chose the correct answer.

1. Are you ready to order?
   A. Yes, I am.
   B. My name is Rob.
   C. Nice to meet you.
   D. What would you like?

2. Would you like something to drink?
   A. Yes. I'd like a green salad.
   B. Yes, I am.
   C. I'll have a tuna sandwich.
   D. Yes, I'd like iced tea, please.

3. Who is the woman?
   A. a customer
   B. a cook
   C. a clerk
   D. a server

4. What does the man start with?
   A. nothing
   B. onion soup
   C. a green salad
   D. some chicken

5. What does the man have for a main course?
   A. a sandwich
   B. a steak
   C. chicken
   D. tuna salad

GRAMMAR AND VOCABULARY: Choose the correct word or phrase to complete each sentence.

6. I need _____ lemons for this recipe.
   A. a little bit of
   B. a few
   C. any
   D. much

7. Can you get _____ milk at the store?
   A. some
   B. much
   C. many
   D. a

8. I have a couple of _____.
   A. milk
   B. rice
   C. juice
   D. eggs

9. How _____ calories are in this dessert?
   A. many
   B. much
   C. any
   D. are

10. How _____ milk do you need?
    A. much
    B. many
    C. any
    D. is

11. There's _____ protein in chicken.
    A. lot of
    B. a lot of
    C. any
    D. many

12. _____ is a dark green vegetable.
   A. Broccoli
   B. A blueberry
   C. A carrot
   D. An onion

13. You buy bananas in _____.
   A. jars
   B. cartons
   C. boxes
   D. bunches

14. I'm on a diet, so I don't want to eat foods with too many _____.
   A. protein
   B. iron
   C. calories
   D. grams

15. _____ is another word for salt.
   A. Sodium
   B. Iron
   C. Gram
   D. Serving

16. An example of a vitamin is _____.
   A. protein
   B. A
   C. fat
   D. calcium

READING: Read the recipe. Then answer the questions.

Cheese and Spinach Omelette (2 servings)

Ingredients	
4 eggs, beaten	1 tbsp. chopped garlic
2 tbsp. olive oil	2 c. spinach leaves
1/2 c. onion, chopped	4 oz. grated cheese
	salt and pepper

Steps
1. First, put the olive oil in a medium-hot frying pan. When the oil is hot, add the chopped onions and garlic. Cook until the onions and garlic are soft.
2. Next, add the spinach leaves and cook them until they get soft.
3. Then add the beaten eggs. Add a little salt and pepper. Turn the heat down and let the eggs cook for about 15 minutes.
4. Finally, add the cheese. Put the eggs in a medium oven until the cheese melts.

17. There are _____ ingredients in this recipe.
   A. five
   B. six
   C. seven
   D. eight

18. There are _____ steps in this recipe.
   A. two
   B. four
   C. five
   D. seven

19. This recipe is for _____ people.
   A. two
   B. three
   C. four
   D. eight

20. This recipe does not contain _____.
   A. vegetables
   B. oil
   C. meat
   D. dairy

Lesson 1

1 MATCH the picture and sentence.

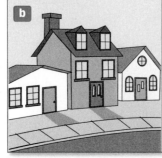

___f___ 1. Pine Street is the busiest street in the neighborhood.

___c___ 2. Oak Street is the quietest street in the neighborhood.

___h___ 3. This is the safest intersection in town.

___g___ 4. This is the most dangerous intersection in town.

___a___ 5. This is the cheapest supermarket in the neighborhood.

___e___ 6. This is the most expensive supermarket in the neighborhood.

___d___ 7. This is the closest school to my house.

___b___ 8. This is the largest house on the street.

2 WRITE the superlative form of each adjective.

1. bad _____the worst_____
2. busy _____the busiest_____
3. expensive _____the most expensive_____
4. large _____the largest_____
5. noisy _____the noisiest_____
6. big _____the biggest_____
7. dangerous _____the most dangerous_____
8. good _____the best_____
9. new _____the newest_____
10. old _____the oldest_____

Lesson 2

1 WRITE. Complete each sentence with the superlative form of the adjective in parentheses.

1. Super Saver market is _____ (cheap) market in town. The food there isn't expensive.

2. Bob's house is _____ (big) house on the street. All the other houses are small.

3. Oak Street Elementary School is _____ (close) school to my house. It's two minutes away.

4. Rob's Café is _____ (good) restaurant in town. It has good food and low prices.

5. The intersection at Green Street and Broadway is _____ (dangerous) intersection in town. There are a lot of accidents there.

2 READ the ads. Then match the abbreviation and the word.

A
Lg. 3 br, 2 ba apt. Sunny kit. W/D in apt. Carpet. Not furn, Gar. No pets. $950/mo.

B
2 br, 1 ba apt. Lg. kit, 2 lg closets, hardwood floors, W/D in building. Pets OK. $850/mo.

C
1 br apt. sm kit, 1 lg closet, lr, dr, Not furn. W/D down the street. Carpet. No pets. $550/mo.

__c__ 1. apartment   _____ 5. kitchen   a. kit   e. furn

_____ 2. bath   _____ 6. large   b. mo   f. W/D

_____ 3. dining room   _____ 7. month   c. apt   g. dr

_____ 4. furnished   _____ 8. washer and dryer   d. ba   h. lg

3 WRITE sentences about the three apartments in Activity 2. Use the words and phrases in the box or your own words.

bathrooms	bedrooms	cheap	closets	expensive	large	small

1. _Apartment C is the cheapest apartment._
2. A most expensive + the biggest
3. B most pet-friendly
4. A is larger than Apt B + C. Apt A is the largest

* which Apt is larger than Apt B?
  " " is the largest? smallest?

Lesson 3

WCD, 48

1 LISTEN to the question. Then listen to the conversation. Fill in the correct answer.

1. Ⓐ   Ⓑ   Ⓒ

2. Ⓐ   Ⓑ   Ⓒ

3. Ⓐ   Ⓑ   Ⓒ

2 WRITE. Complete the conversation. Use the information in the apartment ad.

A: Hello. I'm calling about

the _____

for rent. Is it still available?

B: Yes, it is.

A: Great. Is it furnished?

B: _____.

A: Is there a garage?

B: _____.

A: Is there a washer and dryer?

B: _____.

A: Is there a _____ ?

B: It's one block away.

A: Are _____ ?

B: Yes, _____.

Classifieds

2 br apt, unfurn, 1-car gar. no W/D.
Laundromat 4 blocks away. Supermarket
1 block away. Hardwood floors.
Pets OK. $750/mo.

3 WRITE. Do the math. Write the answers on the lines.

1. What is 20% of $1,550? _____

2. What is 30% of $2,555? _____

3. What is 30% of $3,350? _____

4. What is 35% of $3,750? _____

5. What is 40% of $4,125? _____

Culture and Communication—*Asking for Clarification*

1 LISTEN to and read the conversation. Then practice it with a partner.

W CD, 49

A: Hello. I'm calling about the three-bedroom house for rent. Is it still available?

B: Yes, it is.

A: Great. Is it furnished?

B: Yes, it is.

A: Is there a garage?

B: Yes, there's a one-car garage.

A: I'm sorry, I didn't hear you.
Did you say "a one-car garage"?

A: That's right.

B: Oh, okay. Thank you.

Useful Expressions

Asking for Clarification
I'm sorry, I didn't hear you/that/what you said.
I'm sorry, I didn't get/catch that.
I'm sorry, could you repeat that?
I'm sorry, I missed what you said.
Would you mind saying that again?
Would you mind repeating that?
Did you say . . . ?

2 WRITE. Complete the conversations. Use expressions from the box. *THERE ARE MORE THAN ONE CORRECT ANSWERS!*

1. The landlord says: The laundromat is four blocks away.

   You didn't understand. You say: *I'm sorry, could you repeat that?*

2. The landlord says: There's a washer and dryer in the building.

   You didn't understand. You say: *Would you mind saying that again?*

3. The landlord says: Cats are okay, but not dogs.

   You didn't understand. You say: *Would you mind repeating that?*

3 WHAT ABOUT YOU? Complete the conversation with your own words. Then practice it with a partner.

A: Great. Is it furnished?

B: *Yes, it is furnished.*

A [*you didn't understand*]: *I'm sorry. Can you repeat that?*

B: *The apartment is furnished.*

A: Is there a garage?

B: *No, there is no garage. There is street parking.*

A: Is there a washer and dryer?

B: *Yes, on the first floor.*

A: Thank you very much.

Lesson 4

1 **MATCH** the question and the answer

<u> e </u> 1. What is the cheapest supermarket in town?

a. The course at the community college.

_____ 2. How much is the rent?

b. Gus's Good Gas.

_____ 3. How much does this chair cost?

c. At 10:00 A.M.

_____ 4. What is the best elementary school in town?

d. Pine Valley Elementary.

_____ 5. Which English course do you attend?

e. Max's Market.

_____ 6. Where is the closest convenience store?

f. $45.00.

_____ 7. When does the department store open today?

g. On Pine Street.

_____ 8. Where do you get gas?

h. $1,200 a month.

2 **WRITE.** Complete the questions. Use the correct form of *be* or *do*.

1. How much _____*is*_____ the late fee?
2. Where ___*do*___ they go to school?
3. Where ___*does*___ this package go?
4. Who ___*is*___ your doctor?
5. Which department store ___*do*___ you like?
6. Which department store ___*is*___ the best?

questions/negative

3 **WRITE.** Unscramble the questions.

1. you / often / buy / do / How / gas / ?
   How often do you buy gas?

2. do / to / station / you / Which / go / gas / usually / ?
   _____

3. buy / you / When / usually / groceries / do / ?
   _____

4. closest / you / is / Which / to / the / store / grocery / ?
   _____

5. the / When / open / today / does / store / grocery / ?
   _____

6. in / is / store / What / town / best / the / department / ?
   _____

Lesson 5

1 MATCH the problem and the person.

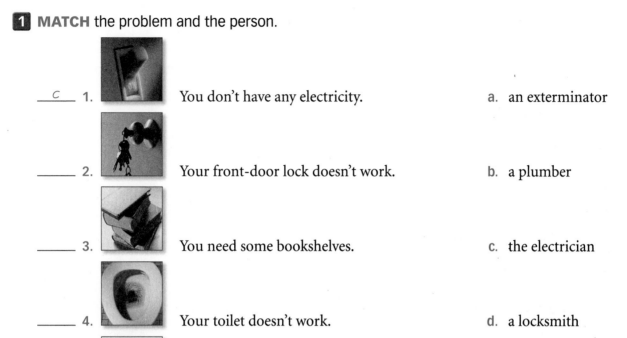

___c___ 1. You don't have any electricity.

a. an exterminator

_____ 2. Your front-door lock doesn't work.

b. a plumber

_____ 3. You need some bookshelves.

c. the electrician

_____ 4. Your toilet doesn't work.

d. a locksmith

_____ 5. You have bugs!

e. a carpenter

2 WRITE. Complete the paragraph. Use the correct form of *be* or *do*.

When (1) ____do____ you call the superintendent? Your building superintendent usually takes care of small problems in your building or your apartment. For more serious problems, you need specialists. For example, who (2) _____ you call when you have electrical problems? You call an electrician. What (3) _____ you do about bugs in your apartment? Call an exterminator. Who (4) _____ the best person to call when you need bookshelves? Call a carpenter. When (5) _____ you call a plumber? Call when you have no hot water or your toilet doesn't flush. And who (6) _____ the best person to call if your front door doesn't lock? If this happens, call a locksmith

3 CIRCLE the word with the most stress in each question.

1. How much does this chair cost?
2. Which plumber do you like?
3. Where is your school?
4. Where is the laundromat?
5. Which stove do you want?
6. Where is the supermarket?

Family Connection—*Understanding Rental Agreements*

1 **READ** the conversation.

Alan: Okay. We have to sign this rental agreement for the apartment. But, first, let's read it carefully.

May: Good idea… The "Parties" in the agreement are the tenant and the landlord and the "Property" is the address of the apartment.

Alan: Yes. And, the apartment also includes the appliances. It includes the refrigerator and the stove.

May: Uh-huh.

Alan: Now, here's the "Term" section. It says that this is a month-to-month rental agreement . . .

May: Well, that's okay. That's better than a lease for us. We can move if we find a better apartment.

Alan: Right. Here's the "Rent" section. We pay $1,250 a month by check on the first day of the month.

May: That's fine.

Alan: Here's the "Utilities" section. We pay for gas and electricity. The landlord pays for garbage collection and water.

May: That's okay. What does it say in the "Deposits" section?

Alan: We have to pay a $500 deposit before we move in.

May: Do we get that money back?

Alan: Yes. We get it back after we move out.

May: What's in the "Additional Terms" section?

Alan: It says the landlord can enter any time . . .

May: Gee, I don't like that . . .

Alan: . . . but she has to give 24 hours' notice.

May: Oh, okay.

2 **CIRCLE** the correct words or phrases.

1. Alan and May are moving into a new **house / apartment.**

2. The "Parties" section includes **the people who sign an agreement** / a description of the apartment.

3. An example of an "appliance" is **a refrigerator** / gas.

4. Alan and May are going to pay their rent once a week / **a month.**

5. Alan and May can pay their rent by credit card / **check.**

6. Alan and May have to pay for **garbage collection and water** / gas and electricity.

7. Alan and May have to pay a deposit of **$500** / $1,250.

8. The landlord can come into Alan and May's apartment any time / **with 24 hours' notice.**

3 **WRITE.** Complete the rental agreement for Alan Wong and May Lee. Check the correct utilities and use the information from the conversation on page 124.

Rental Agreement

1. Parties
The parties to this agreement are ___Susan Patel___ hereinafter called "landlord," and ___Alan Wong + May Lee___ hereinafter called "tenant." If landlord is the agent of the owner of said property, the owner's name and address is:
___Robert Green, Grand Properties, 34585 A Street, San Diego, CA 92101___

2. Property
Landlord hereby lets the following property to tenant for the term of this agreement: (a) the real property known as:
___440 East H Street, Apt. 101, Chula Vista, CA 91910___
And (b) the following furniture and appliances on said property:
___refrigerator and the stove___

3. Term
This agreement shall run from ___month-to-month___ beginning on: ___January 15th, 2009 2018___

4. Rent
The monthly rental for said property shall be $___1250___, due and payable by check by the ___first day___ day of each month.

5. Utilities
Landlord agrees to furnish the following services and/or utilities: ( ) electricity, ( ) gas, (✓) garbage collection, (✓) water.

6. Deposits
Tenant will pay the following deposits and/or fees: ___$500___

This amount will be refunded within three weeks following the termination of the tenancy; unpaid rent, charges for damages beyond normal wear and tear, and costs for reasonable cleaning may be deducted.

Additional Terms
7. Tenant shall not lease, sublease or assign the premises without the prior written consent of the landlord (but this consent shall not be withheld unreasonably).
8. Landlord may enter the premises at reasonable times for the purpose of inspection, maintenance or repair, and to show the premises to buyers or prospective tenants. In all instances, except those of emergency or abandonment, the landlord shall give tenant reasonable notice (at least one day) prior to such an entry.
9. Tenant shall not lease, sublease or assign the premises without the prior written consent of the landlord (but this consent shall not be withheld unreasonably).
10. Landlord may enter the premises at reasonable times for the purpose of inspection, maintenance or repair, and to show the premises to buyers or prospective tenants. In all instances, except those of emergency or abandonment, the landlord shall give tenant reasonable notice (at least one day). Tenant shall not lease, sublease or assign the premises without the prior written consent of the landlord (but this consent shall not be withheld unreasonably), except those of emergency or abandonment, the landlord shall give tenant reasonable notice (at least one day).
11. Landlord may enter the premises for the purpose of inspection, maintenance or repair, and to show the premises to buyers or prospective tenants. In all instances, except those of emergency or abandonment, the landlord shall give tenant reasonable notice (at least one day).

We, the undersigned, agree to this Rental Agreement:

Landlord: Tenant:

___Susan Patel___   ___Alan Wong and May Lee___
Signature   Signature
___1/29/2017___   ___11/29/2017___
Date   Date

---

4 **WHAT ABOUT YOU?** Answer the questions. Write complete sentences.

1. Do you live in an apartment or a house? Do you rent or own it? _____

2. If you rent, do you have a month-to-month rental agreement or a lease? _____

3. Are the stove and refrigerator included in the agreement? _____

4. What utilities are included in your rental agreement? _____

5 **TAKE IT OUTSIDE.** Ask a family member or a friend about their rental agreement. What are the terms?

Community Connection — *Understanding Utility Bills*

1 **READ** the information. Check ☑ the boxes.

What uses gas? What uses electricity?			
	Gas	**Electricity**	**Either gas or electricty**
computer	☐	☐	☐
dryer	☐	☐	☐
refrigerator	☐	☐	☐
stove	☐	☐	☐
water heater	☐	☐	☐

2 **WHAT ABOUT YOU?** What uses gas and electricity in your house or apartment? Complete the chart.

	Gas	**Electricity**
computer	☐	☐
dryer	☐	☐
refrigerator	☐	☐
stove	☐	☐
water heater	☐	☐
[other appliance]	☐	☐

3 **LOOK AND CIRCLE.** Look at Alan's electric bill. Circle these things on the bill.

Alan's address	his name	the account number
the amount to pay	the date he needs to pay	the name of the company

---

YOUR POWER COMPANY   YPC 1001 Power Plane Rd. Energy, CA 90001

Customer
Alan Wong
440 E. H St #101
Chula Vista, CA 91910

Account Number
432115003951

Billing Period
Jan. 15, 2010 – Feb. 14, 2010

Rate	Previous Reading	Present Reading	Units	Unit Cost	Amount
Residential	975420	969430	523 ×	$.11/kwh	57.23
Taxes:					2.09

Payable upon receipt. Please pay your current month charges before 02/27/10.

Customer Information: 800 555 2877
To Report a Power Outage: 800 555 2300

Total Amount Due
$59.62

4 CIRCLE *yes* or *no*.

1. Alan needs to pay $57.62.   **yes**   **no**

2. Alan should pay the bill before January 27, 2010.   **yes**   **no**

3. For questions about his electric bill, Alan calls (800) 555-2877. **yes**   **no**

4. When the electricity goes out, Alan calls (800) 555-2877.   **yes**   **no**

5. Alan used more electricity this month than he did last month.   **yes**   **no**

5 READ AND CIRCLE. Alan wants to lower his electricity bill. He found a list of things to do on the web. Read the list. Then answer the questions.

Need To **KNOW INFO** — Business & Finances   www.needtoknowinfo.com

Autos
Business & Finance
Cities & Towns
Computing & Technology
Education
Electronics & Gadgets
Entertainment
Food & Drink
Health
Hobbies & Games
Home & Garden
Jobs & Careers

SAVING MONEY ON YOUR HOME UTILITES.

To save money, try the following tips:

• Keep the temperature of your water heater low.

• Keep the temperature in your house or apartment low. Wear a sweater instead.

• Keep your heater clean. It works better, and this can save money.

• Use the "Energy Saver" buttons on your dishwasher, washer, and dryer. This way, your appliances use less energy.

• Buy new "Energy Saver" appliances. Old appliances use more energy.

1. What should Alan do with his water heater? _____

2. Why should Alan wear a sweater? _____

3. What should Alan do with his heater? Why? _____

4. What do Energy Saver buttons do? _____

5. Should Alan buy new appliances? Why? _____

6 TAKE IT OUTSIDE. Ask a family member about household appliances and items that use electricity. Make a list of them.

Appliance or Item	Where is it? (What room)	How many?

Career Connection—*Using an Agent to Find an Apartment*

1 READ. Oscar called Boris, a real estate agent. Read their conversation.

> *Boris:* Nikitin Agency, Boris speaking.
>
> *Oscar:* Hi, Boris. Sofia suggested that I call you. I'm looking for an apartment.
>
> *Boris:* Sure. I'd be happy to help. What are you looking for?
>
> *Oscar:* I'm looking for a two-bedroom apartment in a nice neighborhood.
>
> *Boris:* I think I have something you might be interested in. It's the Pine Apartments.
>
> *Oscar:* Are there many families with children in the building?
>
> *Boris:* Yes, lots of families live there.
>
> *Oscar:* Is it a safe neighborhood?
>
> *Boris:* Yes. There isn't much crime. And it's near an elementary school and a park.
>
> *Oscar:* That sounds great. What about public transportation?
>
> *Boris:* The Number 3 bus stops right at the corner.
>
> *Oscar:* Oh, that's great.

2 CIRCLE *yes* or *no*.

1. Oscar wants a three-bedroom apartment.	yes	(no)
2. There are a lot of families in the Pine Apartments.	(yes)	no
3. There's a lot of crime in the neighborhood.	yes	(no)
4. One bus stops near the building.	(yes)	no
5. Oscar is interested in seeing the apartment.	(yes)	no

3 WHAT ABOUT YOU? You are looking for a new apartment. What is important to you? Number the items from 1 to 4. "1" is very important to you. "4" is not important to you. Explain your answers.

Items	Importance (1–4)	Why?
a safe neighborhood (low / no crime)	1	
to be near work	1	
to be near schools	1	
to be near public transportation	3	

Technology Connection: Using Online Apartment Locators

Oscar found a website that lists apartments. Oscar completed a questionnaire. He described the kind of apartment he wanted. Then the website listed all the available apartments.

A **LOOK AND WRITE.** Put the steps in order for an online apartment search.

```
⊗ ⊖ ⊕                        www.myapartment.com

                                    myapartment.com

    Search Rentals    Moving Help    Apartment Tips

    Price:                  Bedrooms:              Type of Housing:
      Min Rent:               ○ Any number           ○ Any
      [$        ]             ○ Studio               ○ Unfurnished
      Max Rent:               ○ One                  ○ Condo/Townhome
      [$        ]             ○ Two                  ○ Campus Area
                              ○ Three                ○ Seniors Community

    Pets:                   Apartment Amenities:
    ○ Cats                    ○ Air conditioning      ○ Hardwood floors
    ○ Small dogs (under 25lbs.)  ○ Balcony/Deck/Patio  ○ High Speed Interent
    ○ Large Dogs              ○ Dishwasher            ○ Washer/Dryer in Unit

    *amenities: Things in a place that make it nice
Done
```

_____ Check the number of bedrooms you want.

_____ Choose the amenities that you want.

_____ Click the "Submit" button.

_____ Type the lowest rent you can pay.

_____ Check the type of housing you want.

_____ Type the highest rent you can pay.

B **PRACTICE.** Do an apartment search. Complete the online questionnaire in Activity A.

Practice Test

LISTENING: Choose the best response. Then listen to the conversation and choose the correct answer.

1. Is the two-bedroom apartment still available?
   A. It's three blocks away.
   B. There's a one-car garage.
   C. Yes, it is.
   D. Cats are O.K.

2. How far is the closest supermarket?
   A. It's two blocks away.
   B. No, there isn't.
   C. Pets are O.K.
   D. There's a washer and dryer.

3. What size apartment is the woman calling about?
   A. a studio
   B. a 1-bedroom apartment
   C. a 2-bedroom apartment
   D. a 3-bedroom apartment

4. Where is the apartment?
   A. on Oak Street
   B. on Green Street
   C. on Block Street
   D. on Pine Street

5. Where is the laundromat?
   A. one block away
   B. two blocks away
   C. three blocks away
   D. four blocks away

GRAMMAR AND VOCABULARY: Choose the correct word or phrase to complete each sentence.

6. Green Park is _____ park in town.
   A. biggest
   B. the biggest
   C. the most
   D. big

7. Market Street is _____ street in the city.
   A. dangerous
   B. most dangerous
   C. the most dangerous
   D. more dangerous

8. Gale's Market is _____ market in the neighborhood.
   A. the best
   B. good
   C. best
   D. better

9. Where _____ the closest park?
   A. is
   B. are
   C. does
   D. do

10. Where _____ you like to shop?
    A. is
    B. are
    C. does
    D. do

11. Where _____ your daughter go to school?
    A. is
    B. are
    C. does
    D. do

12. How much _____ these chairs?
   A. is
   B. are
   C. does
   D. do

13. This apartment doesn't have furniture. It's _____.
   A. furnished
   B. unfurnished
   C. furniture
   D. hardwood floors

14. The opposite of *safe* is _____.
   A. quiet
   B. cheap
   C. dangerous
   D. expensive

15. The opposite of *expensive* is _____.
   A. cheap
   B. quiet
   C. safe
   D. dangerous

16. A person who kills bugs is _____.
   A. a carpenter
   B. an electrician
   C. a locksmith
   D. an exterminator

READING: Read the article. Then answer the questions.

Is your electric bill too high? Do you want to save money? There are several things you can do to lower your electric bill each month. Here are some suggestions: Dryers use a lot of electricity. Dry your clothes outside instead. You can save money and your clothes smell better, too! Turn off lights when you are not in a room. And don't turn on lights in the daytime. Let the sun light your rooms! Is the heater on a lot? Maybe cold air is coming through your windows and doors. Replace old windows. Close up the gaps—those open spaces—around your doors. This will keep your place much warmer. And don't forget to turn down your heater at night. It saves money, and it's also healthier.

17. What is the main idea of the article?
   A. ways to stay healthy
   B. ways to save money
   C. ways to lower your electricity bill
   D. ways to fix your windows and doors

18. There are _____ suggestions in this article.
   A. two
   B. four
   C. five
   D. six

19. What does the article suggest?
   A. Turn lights on during the day.
   B. Dry your clothes outside.
   C. Replace new windows.
   D. Turn up the heater at night.

20. Gaps around doors _____.
   A. let cold air in
   B. lower your electricity bill
   C. keep your house warm
   D. are healthy

LESSON 1

1 MATCH the parts of the sentences. Write the letters.

_____f____ 1. Juan has to fill out   a. expired last week.

_____ 2. Maria has to take   b. to Window 13.

_____ 3. I have to renew   c. license.

_____ 4. Ann has to practice   d. test.

_____ 5. Sam wants to get a driver's   e. my license.

_____ 6. Marta has to take a driving   f. an application.

_____ 7. I have to go   g. driving.

_____ 8. Dimitri's license   h. a written test.

2 WRITE. Complete the sentences with the correct form of *have to*.

1. Wei and Lucy _____ go to the Department of Motor Vehicles.

2. Mark _____ get a driver's license this week.

3. Sue _____ (not) fill out an application.

4. You _____ go to Window 13.

5. Sofia _____ take her written test today.

6. Dan and I _____ (not) practice driving this afternoon.

3 READ AND WRITE. Look at Tim's schedule. Write sentences with *has to* and *doesn't have to*.

Monday	Tuesday	Wednesday	Thursday	Friday
• go to school • go to work	• go to school • go to work • practice driving	• go to school • take a test • no work today	• go to school • go to work • exercise	• no school today • go to work • get a driver's license

1. _On Monday, Tim has to go to school._____

2. _____

3. _____

4. _____

5. _____

LESSON 2

1 WRITE. Complete the sentences. Use *must* or *must not* for a rule. Use *should* or *should not* for a suggestion.

1. Mari can't see the doctor without an appointment. (rule) She _____*must*_____ make an appointment.

2. Sam's Café has great food. (suggestion) You _____ eat there.

3. There's a "No Left Turn" sign. (rule) He _____ turn left here.

4. Nick doesn't want to walk to work. (suggestion) He _____ get a driver's license.

5. This road is dangerous. (rule) Drivers _____ be careful.

6. You're tired. (suggestion) You _____ work too late.

7. There's a test tomorrow. (rule) You _____ be late.

8. Rob wants to lose weight. (suggestion) He _____ exercise every day.

2 WRITE sentences about the signs. Use *must* or *must not*.

1. _____

2. _____

3. _____

4. _____

5. _____

6. _____

LESSON 3

1 **LISTEN** to the question. Then listen to the conversation. Fill in the correct answer.

WCD, 51

1. Ⓐ   Ⓑ   Ⓒ

2. Ⓐ   Ⓑ   Ⓒ

3. Ⓐ   Ⓑ   Ⓒ

2 **CIRCLE** the words that you hear.

WCD, 52

1. has a / has to   6. has a / has to

2. have a / have to   7. has a / has to

3. has a / has to   8. have a / have to

4. has a / has to   9. has a / has to

5. have a / have to   10. has a / has to

3 **WRITE.** Put the lines of the conversation in the correct order. The first line is done for you.

B: Okay. Thank you.

A: First, you have to fill out an application.

A: Hi. Can I help you?

A: Yes, you do.

B: Do I have to take a written test?

B: Yes, I'd like to apply for a learner's permit. What do I have to do?

Practice Role Play!

A: *Hi. Can I help you?* _____

B: _____

A: _____

B: _____

A: _____

B _____

Culture and Communication — *Making Suggestions*

WCD, 53

1 **LISTEN AND READ.** Listen to and read the conversations. Then practice them with a partner.

1

A: I have to get a driver's license, but I don't know how to drive.
B: How about taking driving lessons?
A: That's a good idea.

2

A: I have to renew my license, but I don't want to wait in a long line!
B: Why don't you make an appointment?
A: That's a great idea!

3

A: I have to get a car, but I don't have much money.
B: You should get a used car.
A: Good idea!

2 **WRITE.** Complete the suggestions.

1. Your friend says: I have to practice driving before I take my test.

   You say: _____ going driving with me today?

2. Your friend says: I have to be at work early tomorrow, and my car doesn't work.

   You say: _____ take the subway?

3. Your friend says: I have to take a big test on Monday.

   You say: _____ study this weekend.

> **Useful Expressions**
>
> **Making Suggestions**
> You should . . .
> You ought to . . .
> Why don't you . . .?
> How about . . .?
> What about. . .?
> I suggest (that) . . .
> I think (that) . . .

3 **READ AND WRITE.** Read the problems. Write conversations with suggestions. Then practice your conversations with a partner.

1. Ana and Diego have to find a new apartment.

   _____

   _____

2. Rob has to take a driving test.

   _____

   _____

3. Sam is driving fast. There's a police officer behind him.

   _____

   _____

LESSON 4

1 READ the sentences. Circle *C* for a command. Circle *S* for a suggestion.

1. Go through the next intersection.   (C)   S
2. Let's walk across the street.   C   S
3. Let's not go down Oak Street.   C   S
4. Drive out of the parking lot.   C   S
5. Don't go into the building.   C   S
6. Let's drive west on Mulberry Street.   C   S
7. Drive away from the library.   C   S
8. Go toward the exit.   C   S

2 WRITE. <u>Underline</u> the direction words in the sentences in Activity 1.

3 WRITE commands or suggestions. Write complete sentences.

1. north on Pine Street (suggestion): _____
2. not turn left here (command): _____
3. turn right at the next intersection (command): _____
4. walk through the park and cross Main Street (suggestion): _____
5. turn left at the intersection (suggestion): _____
6. not drive into that parking lot (command): _____

4 READ AND WRITE. Read the situation. Write an affirmative or a negative command.

1. Your friend is going the wrong way down the street. (negative) _____

_____

2. Your friend wants to park the car. You see a parking lot. (affirmative) _____

_____

3. Your friend is driving too fast. (affirmative) _____

_____

4. Your friend is running a stop sign. (negative) _____

_____

5. Your friend is turning right. There is a "No Right Turn" sign. (negative) _____

_____

LESSON 5

1 **MATCH** the person and the sentence.

_____ 1. Go under the overpass.

_____ 2. Walk past the library.

_____ 3. Go around the school.

_____ 4. Cross the street.

_____ 5. Walk over the overpass.

_____ 6. Drive over the bridge.

2 **LOOK AND WRITE.** Look at the map. Kim lives at 345 Orange Street. His building is at the intersection of Orange and Pine, on the northwest corner. Find it and write "Kim's Apartment" on the map. Then write directions from Kim's apartment to the places below.

Kim wants to go to

1. Millie's Restaurant (F) _____

_____

2. the school (A) _____

_____

3. the DMV (D) _____

_____

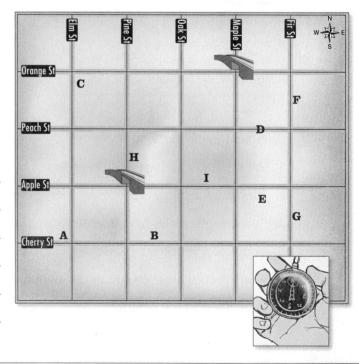

Family Connection—*Getting Auto Insurance*

1 READ. Alan and May bought a car. Now they need to get car insurance. Read the definitions. Then read the article on car insurance companies.

> **claim:** a request for payment from an insurance company after an accident, for example
>
> **collision insurance:** insurance that covers car repairs after an accident
>
> **coverage:** the general term for the amount of insurance and the kinds of problems that the insurance pays for
>
> **deductible:** the amount of money you must pay on a claim before your insurance company pays anything
>
> **discount:** paying less than the full amount of money for insurance coverage
>
> **make:** the name of the company that made your car; for example, Toyota
>
> **model:** the type of car that you have; for example, a Corolla
>
> **policy:** a written agreement between a car insurance company and a driver
>
> **quote:** the price you will pay for insurance, given to you by the company and before you sign a policy

Everyone who drives must have car insurance. How do you find a car insurance company?

Follow these steps:

1. First, answer these questions:
   - How much coverage do you need? Do you want collision insurance? Do you want a large deductible or a small one?
   - Do you have an expensive car? Do you have a bank loan on the car? You might need a lot of coverage.
   - Do you have any recent tickets or accidents? If yes, your insurance will cost more.

2. Next, go online and compare policies. For online insurance websites, you will need to give information about yourself and your car's make and model. You can get quotes online. Print them out to make it easy to compare companies and prices.

3. Look for discounts. For example, you can get a discount when you get insurance for more than one car. You can get a discount for car alarms and other anti-theft devices. You can even get discounts for the type of job you have.

4. Then choose the best company for you. Get recommendations. For example, car repair shops know a lot about insurance companies. Ask them for recommendations. What happens after an accident? Is it easy to contact the company when you have a claim?

5. Finally, read your policy carefully before you sign it. An insurance policy is a legal document. Know what your insurance covers and what it does not cover.

2 CIRCLE *yes* or *no*.

1. All drivers must have car insurance.	(yes)	no
2. Tickets make your car insurance less expensive.	yes	no
3. You can get quotes for car insurance online.	yes	no
4. Some people can get a discount on their car insurance.	yes	no
5. Construction workers usually know a lot about car insurance companies.	yes	no
6. A policy is a kind of agreement.	yes	no

3 WRITE. Alan wants to get some quotes from car insurance companies. Help him fill in part of an online form. Complete the form with the words and phrases in the box.

12,000 miles per year	Alan Wong	cook	Toyota
to commute to work or school	March 25, 1985	91910	1999

⊗ ⊖ ⊕   www.insurancecomparison.com

Please fill out the form below.

About You

Your name: [   ]

Your date of birth: [   ]

Gender: Male ⦿   Female ○   Your ZIP code: [   ]

Do you currently have insurance?   Yes ○   No ⦿

Have you had a driver's license for more than 3 years?   Yes ⦿   No ○

Have you had any accidents in the past 3 years?   Yes ○   No ⦿

Occupation [   ]

About Your Car

Year: [   ]   Make: [   ]   Model: [Corrolla]

What do you use the car for? [   ]

How many miles do you drive each year? [   ]

---

4 WHAT ABOUT YOU? Fill in the form with your own information. If you don't have a car, think about the car you want to have.

⊗ ⊖ ⊕   www.insurancecomparison.com

Please fill out the form below.

About You

Your name: [   ]

Your date of birth: [   ]

Gender: Male ○   Female ○   Your ZIP code: [   ]

Do you currently have insurance?   Yes ○   No ○

Have you had a driver's license for more than 3 years?   Yes ○   No ○

Have you had any accidents in the past 3 years?   Yes ○   No ○

Occupation [   ]

About Your Car

Year: [   ]   Make: [   ]   Model: [   ]

What do you use the car for? [   ]

How many miles do you drive each year? [   ]

Community Connection—*Getting a Driver's License*

1 **READ.** Ann Lee has to get a driver's license. She went to the DMV website and found out about the steps. Read the steps.

---

www.dmv.org

Driver License Information for Persons Over 18

• Applying for a driver license over 18
• Applying for a (CDL)
• Applying for a motorcycle or moped license

CALIFORNIA
DRIVER'S LICENSE

Provisional Driver Permit Under 18

• Applying for a provisional permit under 18
• Driver Education and
• Training Information
• Restrictions during the first year
• Teen Driver Information

How to apply for a Driver License if you are over 18

Step 1: Visit a DMV office. Call 924-555-9045 to make an appointment, or make an appointment online.
Step 2: Fill out an application. Don't forget your Social Security number.
Step 3: Have your picture taken.
Step 4: Pay a fee of $27.00.
Step 5. Pass an eye exam.
Step 6: Pass a written test. Study the Driver's Handbook. You can take practice tests online.
Step 7: Pass a driving test.
Step 8: Give information about your car insurance.

How to apply for a Commercial Drivers License (CDL)

Done

---

2 **CIRCLE** *yes* or *no*.

1. Ann can get a driver's license over the phone.   yes   (no)

2. She has to take two tests.   yes   no

3. She can take a practice test online.   yes   no

4. She has to pay $25 to get a driver's license.   yes   no

5. She needs car insurance to get a driver's license.   yes   no

---

3 **MATCH.** Ann got her driver's license. Match the parts of the license and her personal information.

___C___ 1. the driver's name

_____ 2. the license number

_____ 3. the driver's address

_____ 4. the driver's photo

_____ 5. the state where the driver lives

_____ 6. the driver's date of birth

_____ 7. the date that the license expires

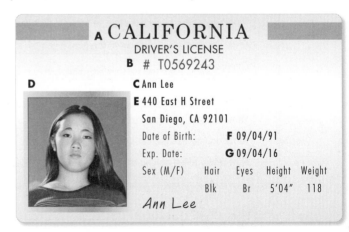

A **CALIFORNIA**
DRIVER'S LICENSE
B # T0569243

D

C Ann Lee
E 440 East H Street
San Diego, CA 92101
Date of Birth: F 09/04/91
Exp. Date: G 09/04/16
Sex (M/F)   Hair   Eyes   Height   Weight
            Blk   Br   5'04"   118

Ann Lee

4 MATCH. Ann is studying the Driver's Handbook. Match the road sign and the meaning.

_____ 1.

_____ 2.

_____ 3.

_____ 4.

_____ 5.

_____ 6.

_____ 7.

_____ 8.

a. There's a traffic signal ahead.

b. There's a place for people to cross the street ahead.

c. Don't make a U-turn here.

d. This road is slippery when it's wet.

e. Don't park here.

f. There's an airport ahead.

g. Don't drive over 55 miles per hour.

h. People are working on the road ahead.

5 TAKE IT OUTSIDE. Find out about the Department of Motor Vehicles in your city. Answer these questions.

1. What is the address of the Department of Motor Vehicles? _____

_____

2. What is the telephone number? _____

_____

3. What do you need to bring if you want to get a license? _____

_____

4. Are there practice tests online? _____

_____

5. (Your own question) _____

_____

Career Connection—*Understanding Maps*

1 **LOOK AND CIRCLE.** Oscar is going to go to Pittsburgh, PA. Look at the map. It shows a large area around Pittsburgh. Circle the answers to the questions.

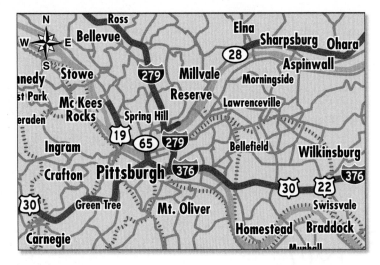

1. What is the name of the biggest city on the map?

   McKees Rocks   Pittsburgh   Wilkinsburg

2. Mt. Oliver is the name of _____.

   a river   a street   a town

3. Spring Hill is _____ of Pittsburgh.

   north   south   east   west

4. Crafton is _____ of Pittsburgh.

   north   south   east   west

2 **WHAT ABOUT YOU?** Describe where you live. Write at least three sentences. Use words from the box.

east	north	south	west
northeast	northwest	southeast	southwest

_____

_____

_____

_____

_____

Technology Connection: Using Online Maps

Oscar used the web to search for pizza restaurants in Pittsburgh.

A **LOOK AND WRITE.** Put the steps in order for an online business search.

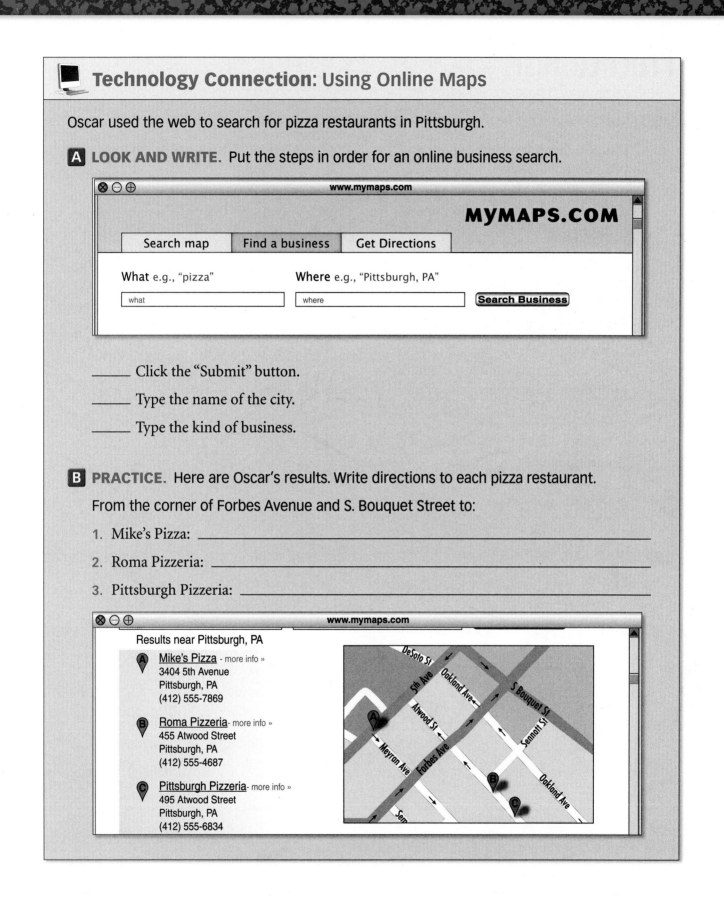

_____ Click the "Submit" button.

_____ Type the name of the city.

_____ Type the kind of business.

B **PRACTICE.** Here are Oscar's results. Write directions to each pizza restaurant.

From the corner of Forbes Avenue and S. Bouquet Street to:

1. Mike's Pizza: _____

2. Roma Pizzeria: _____

3. Pittsburgh Pizzeria: _____

Practice Test

LISTENING: Choose the best response. Then listen to the conversation and choose the correct answer.

1. I'd like to renew my driver's license. What do I have to do?
   A. O.K. Thank you.
   B. You have to fill out an application.
   C. No, you don't.
   D. Do I have to take a driving test?

2. Do you know how to get to the DMV?
   A. No, you don't.
   B. You have to fill out an application.
   C. It's $25.
   D. Yes. Go north on Elm Street and turn right on Peach.

3. Who is the woman?
   A. a police officer
   B. a teacher
   C. a passenger
   D. a DMV worker

4. How much does the man have to pay?
   A. $12
   B. $27
   C. $37
   D. $47

5. Where does the man have to go?
   A. Window 2
   B. Window 11
   C. Window 12
   D. Window 27

GRAMMAR AND VOCABULARY: Choose the correct word or phrase to complete each sentence.

6. Sam _____ to renew his driver's license.
   A. have
   B. is
   C. has
   D. must

7. Ann and Amy _____ to go to the DMV today.
   A. has
   B. having
   C. have
   D. must

8. You _____ not turn left here.
   A. must
   B. have
   C. has
   D. don't

9. You have a test on Monday. You _____ study this weekend.
   A. do
   B. have
   C. has
   D. should

10. Let's _____ down Pine Street.
    A. walking
    B. walk
    C. walked
    D. walks

11. _____ over the bridge and then turn right on Main Street.
    A. Goes
    B. Go
    C. Going
    D. Went

12. _____ park here!
   A. Don't
   B. Doesn't
   C. Doing
   D. Did

13. The opposite of *away from* is _____.
   A. out of
   B. toward
   C. under
   D. through

14. The opposite of *into* is _____.
   A. toward
   B. north
   C. down
   D. out of

15. The opposite of *north* is _____.
   A. south
   B. east
   C. west
   D. up

16. When you *renew* a license, you _____.
   A. get a ticket
   B. get a new one
   C. stop driving
   D. get pulled over

READING: Read the email. Then answer the questions.

www.emailme.com

(10) Inbox	From:	Sara Green
(1) Draft	To:	English Class
	Subject:	Class Party
	Date:	June 11, 2011 5:05 P.M.

(5) Sent

(8) Bulk

Trash

Dear Class,
Next Friday is the last day of class, so we're having a class party. We're having it at my house. Don't forget to bring some food! Here are the directions:

Start at the school and go north on Elm Street toward the movie theater. Don't go past the shoe store. Turn left on Peach Street, pass the fire station, and then turn left on Oak Street. Don't go over the overpass. Walk up Oak until you get to Orange Street. Cross Orange Street. My house is on the northeast corner of Oak Street and Orange Street. It's 127 Oak Street.

Sara

17. What is the email about?
   A. directions to the movie theater
   B. what to bring to a party
   C. food for a class party
   D. directions to a class party

18. Where does Sara live?
   A. on Orange Street
   B. on the northeast corner of Orange Street and Oak Street
   C. on the northwest corner of Orange Street and Oak Street
   D. on the northeast corner of Peach Street and Elm Street

19. Why is Sara having a party?
   A. to celebrate her birthday
   B. to celebrate a holiday
   C. to celebrate the first day of class
   D. to celebrate the last day of class

20. What are people bringing to the party?
   A. food
   B. gifts
   C. music
   D. games

LESSON 1

1 **WRITE.** Complete the sentences with the correct form of *be + going to*.

1. Wei and Lucy _____ *are going to* _____ go out on Friday night.
2. Mark _____ (not) go out on Friday night.
3. I _____ go hiking on Sunday.
4. You _____ (not) study this weekend.
5. Sofia _____ (not) stay home tomorrow.
6. We _____ go dancing on Saturday night.
7. Amy and Ana _____ (not) go running this weekend.
8. Dan _____ work on a project this Saturday.

2 **WRITE.** Unscramble the questions.

1. to / Is / Lucy / go / going / Saturday / on / hiking / ?
   Is Lucy going to go hiking on Saturday? _____

2. you / this / going / What / weekend / are / do / to / ?
   _____

3. invite / is / going / Mari / Who / dinner / to / for / over / ?
   _____

4. Maria / project / going / work / Saturday / Is / to / a / on / this / ?
   _____

5. dancing / When / go / are / going / you / to / ?
   _____

6. night / you / to / home / going / stay / are / tomorrow / Why / ?
   _____

3 **WRITE** answers to the questions. Write complete sentences.

1. What are you going to do tonight? _____
2. Where are you going to go tomorrow? _____
3. What are you going to do this weekend? _____
4. Where are you going to go this Saturday? _____

LESSON 2

1 **WRITE** questions and answers about the pictures. Use the correct form of *be + going to*.

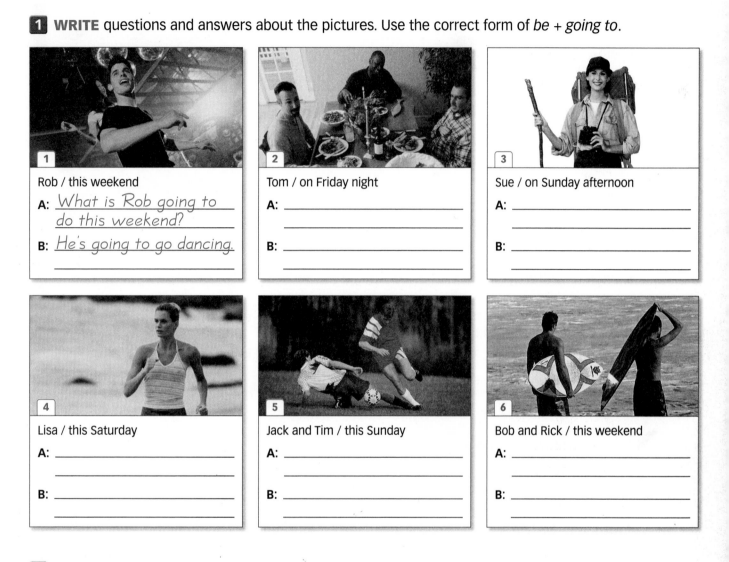

1

Rob / this weekend

A: *What is Rob going to do this weekend?*

B: *He's going to go dancing.*

2

Tom / on Friday night

A: _____

_____

B: _____

_____

3

Sue / on Sunday afternoon

A: _____

_____

B: _____

_____

4

Lisa / this Saturday

A: _____

_____

B: _____

_____

5

Jack and Tim / this Sunday

A: _____

_____

B: _____

_____

6

Bob and Rick / this weekend

A: _____

_____

B: _____

_____

2 **WRITE.** Complete the paragraph with the correct form of *be + going to*.

My family (1) _____ do a lot of different things this weekend. On Saturday, my mother (2) _____ work on a project at home. My father (3) _____ go shopping in the afternoon. Then my parents (4) _____ have friends over for dinner on Saturday night. I (5) _____ go to a soccer game on Saturday, and I (6) _____ go to a movie on Saturday night. My brother has a big test on Monday. He (7) _____ study this weekend, but he and his friends (8) _____ play computer games on Saturday night. On Sunday, (9) I _____ sleep in. Then, my friends and I (10) _____ go to the beach on Sunday afternoon.

LESSON 3

1 LISTEN. Circle *now* or *future*.

WCD, 55

1. now   future

2. now   future

3. now   future

4. now   future

5. now   future

6. now   future

7. now   future

8. now   future

9. now   future

10. now   future

2 LISTEN to the question. Then listen to the conversation. Fill in the correct answer.

WCD, 56

1. Ⓐ   Ⓑ   Ⓒ

2. Ⓐ   Ⓑ   Ⓒ

3. Ⓐ   Ⓑ   Ⓒ

3 WRITE. Complete the conversation. Use the words and phrases in the box.

a nice weekend	are going to go	go shopping
hiking	I'm going to	this weekend

A: What are you going to do _____?

B: I'm going to _____ on Saturday.

On Sunday, I'm going to go _____.

How about you?

A: My friends and I _____ to a movie on

Saturday night. And _____ go to a soccer

game on Sunday.

B: Oh, that sounds like _____.

Culture and Communication — *Making, Accepting, and Refusing Invitations*

WCD, 57

1 LISTEN AND READ. Listen to and read the conversations. Then practice them with a partner.

> *Maria:* Would you like to go to a movie with me on Saturday night?
>
> *Mark:* Sure. That sounds nice.

> *Lisa:* Hi, Raul. Would you like to go to a movie with me on Saturday night?
>
> *Raul:* Oh, thanks, but I'm busy Saturday night.

Useful Expressions		
Making Invitations	**Accepting Invitations**	**Refusing Invitations**
Would you like to . . .	Yes, thank you. I'd love/like to.	No, thanks. I'm busy. I'm . . .
Do you want to . . .	Thank you. I'd love/like to.	No, thanks. I'd rather not./I'd rather . . .
	Thanks. That sounds great/nice.	Thanks, but I'm . . . .
	Sure. Thanks.	

2 WRITE. Complete the conversations. Use expressions from the box.

1. *A:* Do you want to go to a soccer game with me on Saturday?

   B: No, _____.

2. *A:* Do you want to go to a movie with me on Saturday night?

   B: Yes, _____.

3. *A:* Would you like to go to a movie with me on Saturday night?

   B: Thanks, but I'm _____.

3 TALK Read about the situations. Practice conversations with a partner.

1. You ask a friend to go dancing on Friday night. Your friend accepts your invitation.

2. You ask a friend over for dinner on Saturday night. Your friend refuses. He/she is busy.

LESSON 4

1 **MATCH** the picture and the celebration.

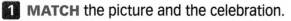

_____ 1. anniversary

_____ 2. birthday

_____ 3. Father's Day

_____ 4. graduation

_____ 5. Independence Day

_____ 6. Mother's Day

_____ 7. President's Day

_____ 8. wedding

2 **READ** and circle *less sure* or *more sure*.

1. We probably won't go out on Friday night.   **less sure**   **more sure**

2. I probably will get married at the beach.   **less sure**   **more sure**

3. My father might visit me this weekend.   **less sure**   **more sure**

4. We may give my mother some flowers.   **less sure**   **more sure**

5. They'll probably go out to dinner tonight.   **less sure**   **more sure**

3 **WRITE.** Complete the sentences with *may, might,* or *will probably* and the verb in parentheses. Use contractions with *will*. More than one answer is possible.

1. Nick _____ (graduate) from college next year.

2. He _____ (celebrate) his birthday at a restaurant.

3. Amy _____ (have) her friends over for dinner this weekend.

4. I _____ (not go dancing) this Saturday.

5. Sara and Sam _____ (get married) in June.

LESSON 5

1 WRITE. Unscramble the sentences.

1. weekend / easy / might / Amy / this / take it / .

   _____

2. will / fireworks / on / I / probably / Independence Day / watch / .

   _____

3. Father's Day / you / going / do / What / on / are / to / ?

   _____

4. picnic / My / afternoon / to / going / friends / are / have / a / this / .

   _____

5. may / house / clean / on / They / the / Saturday / .

   _____

6. Dave / go / afternoon / on / may / Saturday / not / shopping / .

   _____

7. Martin / on / not / go / and / out / night / Lucy / might / Saturday / .

   _____

8. the / won't / beach / afternoon / They / to / go / probably / Sunday / on /.

   _____

2 WRITE. Look at Marta's schedule. Then complete the sentences with *going to, may, might,* or *will probably*. The question marks show things that Marta might do.

Monday	Tuesday	Wednesday	Thursday	Friday	Saturday/Sunday
President's Day Go to the beach?	English class, 10:00 A.M. to 12 noon	Have lunch with Raul? Work, 1:00 P.M. to 6:00 P.M.	English class, 10:00 A.M. to 12 noon Work, 1:00 P.M. to 6:00 P.M.	Study at the library? Work, 1:00 P.M. to 6:00 P.M.	Play soccer Go to a movie with Amy?

1. _____*Marta might*_____ go to the beach on Monday.

2. _____ work on Wednesday.

3. _____ have lunch with Raul on Wednesday.

4. _____ go to English class on Thursday.

5. _____ study at the library on Friday.

6. _____ go to a movie with Amy on the weekend.

Family Connection—*Planning Family Activities*

1 **MATCH** the word and the picture.

_____ 1. aerobics   _____ 3. seniors   _____ 5. weight training

_____ 2. bingo   _____ 4. theater

2 **READ** the list of classes and activities in a community center catalog. Ciricle *yes* or *no*.

🏕 Pine Valley Community Center

567 Pine Valley Avenue, Pine Valley, CA
415-555-6879
www.pinevalleycenter.org

Adult and Teen Classes	**Children's Classes**	**Activities for Seniors**
Art	Art	Exercise for Seniors
Music	Music	Driving Review
Tennis	Theater	Bingo
	Tennis	

Swimming Classes   **Fitness Center Programs**
Children   Aerobics
Adults   Dance
Water Aerobics   Weight Training
Swim Lessons for Seniors

The Community Center is open
Monday-Saturday 9:00 A.M.-5:00 P.M.

The Community Center is closed on holidays

The pool and fitness center are open
Monday-Thursday 6:30 A.M. to 9:00 P.M.
Saturday 7:30 A.M.-5:00 P.M.
Sunday 8:30 A.M.-5:00 P.M.

1. Adults and teens can take music classes.   yes   no

2. Adults and teens can take theater classes.   yes   no

3. Children can play bingo.   yes   no

4. Children can take tennis lessons.   yes   no

5. Grandparents can find something to do.   yes   no

6. You can learn how to swim.   yes   no

7. The website for the community center is www.pinevalleycenter.net.   yes   no

8. You can go swimming on Sunday.   yes   no

9. The community center is closed on Veteran's Day.   yes   no

3 **WRITE.** Look at the community center catalog. Find a class or activity for each person.

Person	Class/Activity
1. Grandma Rose: 70 years old; likes to play games	
2. Linda: 35 years old; wants to get some exercise; likes dance	
3. Mark: 40 year old; wants to get some exercise, likes water	
4. Lisa: 14 years old; wants to learn a new sport	
5. Rob: 8 years old; wants to be an actor when he grows up	

4 **READ AND CIRCLE.** Look at the Pine Valley Community Center pool schedule. Circle the correct answer.

	Monday	Tuesday	Wednesday	Thursday	Friday	Saturday	Sunday
7:00 A.M.	Water Aerobics						Closed
8:00 A.M.							
9:00 A.M.	Family Swim						Open Swim
10:00 A.M.							
11:00 A.M.							
NOON							
1:00 P.M.	Swim Lessons	Water Aerobics	Swim Lessons for Seniors	Water Aerobics	Swim Lessons	Swim Lessons	
2:00 P.M.							
3:00 P.M.							
4:00 P.M.	Family Swim	Swim Lessons	Family Swim	Swim Lessons	Family Swim	Pool Closed	
5:00 P.M.							
6:00 P.M.							
7:00 P.M.	Water Aerobics		Water Aerobics				
8:00 P.M.							

1. The Lee family can swim together on Friday at **3:00 P.M. / 6:00 P.M.**

2. The Lee family can't swim together at 4:00 P.M. on **Friday / Saturday**.

3. Rob Lee can take a swim lesson at 1:00 P.M. on **Thursday / Saturday**.

4. Mark Lee can take a water aerobics class on Monday at **7:00 P.M. / 1:00 P.M.**

5. Lisa Lee can take a **water aerobics class / swim lesson** on Saturday at 7:00 A.M.

6. Grandma Rose can take a swim lesson on Wednesday at **1:00 P.M. / 4:00 P.M.**

Community Connection—*Volunteering*

1 **READ** the article.

Why do people volunteer?

Volunteering—why do people do it? Volunteers help build and repair houses. They take food to sick people. They teach seniors how to use computers. They clean up beaches and parks. And they don't get paid! Why do so many people volunteer?

There are many reasons. Some people like to help other people. They say it makes them feel good. Some people say an organization or a community helped them in the past, and now they want to "give something back." Other people volunteer as a way to make new friends. And some people volunteer to get job experience. Their reasons are different, but volunteers are the same in one way: they are very important. We need them. Our world is a much better place, thanks to volunteers.

Volunteers clean up Pine Valley Park

2 **WRITE.** Complete the chart with information from the article.

Examples of Volunteer Jobs	Reasons People Volunteer
help build and repair houses	

3 **READ** the list of volunteer jobs.

Search Opportunities **VolunteerStuff.org** Home Matching Emergency Response Nonprofits Newletter

Zip Code

Distance

Interest Area

(Search) Advanced Search

◯ **Volunteering**

◯ **Donating**

◯ **Contact Us**

Organization	Job	Time & Requirements	Good for
The Pine Valley Animal Shelter	Take care of animals	3 hours per week	kids, teens
The Pine Valley Senior Center	Deliver food to seniors at home	5 hours per week; must be over 18	adults
Homes for Everyone	Help built and repair houses for poor people	8 hours each weekend; must have a driver's license	teens, adults
Pine Valley Elementary School	Help children learn to use computers	5 hours per week	teens, adults, seniors
Pine Valley School District	Set up computers; install software; repair computers	10 hours per week	teens, adults, seniors
Pine Valley Parks and Recreation	Clean up Pine Valley Park	This Saturday, November 3, 8:00 A.M. to 5:00 P.M.	all ages

4 CIRCLE the correct word or words.

1. The Pine Valley Animal Shelter job is a good job for **kids / seniors**.

2. The Pine Valley Senior Center job is good for **adults / teens**.

3. You **do / do not** have to drive for the Homes for Everyone job.

4. At Pine Valley Elementary School, volunteers help **children / seniors** learn to use computers.

5. You probably **do / do not** have to know about computers for the Pine Valley School District job.

6. The job for Pine Valley Parks and Recreation is **every / this** Saturday.

5 WRITE. Find a volunteer job from Activity 3 for these people. Write the name of the organization on the line.

1. A volunteer helped Carlos repair his house in the past. Now, he wants to "give something back."

   A good job for him is at _____.

2. Sam is 8 years old. He loves animals. A good job for him is at _____.

3. Amy is 16. She likes to repair computers, and she wants to work with computers someday.

   A good job for her is at _____.

4. Wei just moved to Pine Valley. He doesn't know anyone, and he works Monday to Friday.

   He wants to make some friends. A good job for him is at _____.

5. Ana is 65 years old. She likes to help children, and she knows a lot about computers.

   A good job for her is at _____.

6. Rob likes to help seniors. A good job for him is at _____.

6 REAL-LIFE LESSON. Find a friend or family member with a volunteer job. Ask these questions, or ask your own questions.

1. What organization do you volunteer for? _____

2. What is your volunteer job? _____

3. What do you do? _____

   _____

4. Why do you volunteer? _____

   _____

Career Connection—*Interpreting Time-Keeping Forms*

1 **READ** Oscar's time card. Circle the time he arrives at work.
Underline the time he leaves work.

Name:	*Oscar Santos*		
Period:	*Ending July 6*		

DATE	Start/In	Stop/Out	Hours Worked
Jul 1	11:21 A.M.	7:31 P.M.	8:10
Jul 2	11:24 A.M.	7:29 P.M.	8:05
Jul 3	11:31 A.M.	7:31 P.M.	8:00
Jul 5	11:15 A.M.	7:45 P.M.	8:30
Jul 6	11:29 A.M.	7:26 P.M.	8:03

Signature _____

2 **CIRCLE** the correct word.

1. This time card is for **June / July** .

2. Oscar worked **five / six** days this week.

3. Oscar probably starts work at **11:30 A.M. / 12:30 P.M.**

4. Oscar usually leaves work at about **7:00 P.M. / 7:30 P.M.**

5. Oscar usually works about **seven / eight** hours a day.

6. Oscar is **worked / did not work** on Independence Day.

3 **WRITE** answers to the questions.

1. How many hours did Oscar work this week? _____

2. On what date didn't Oscar work this week? _____

3. What holiday is on that date? _____

4. What are probably Oscar's regular working hours? _____

5. Why might Oscar sometimes stay late? _____

_____

Technology Connection: Using an Electronic Time Clock

Workers at the restaurant use a mechanical time clock. Some workplaces use electronic time clocks.

LOOK at the electronic time clock and the swipe card. Match the words and the letters.

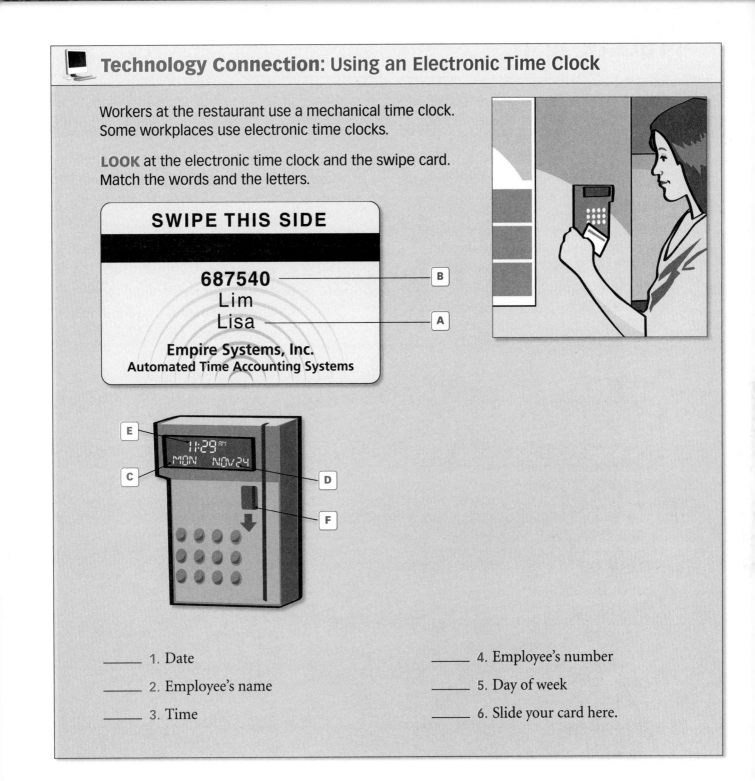

_____ 1. Date

_____ 2. Employee's name

_____ 3. Time

_____ 4. Employee's number

_____ 5. Day of week

_____ 6. Slide your card here.

Practice Test

LISTENING: Choose the best response. Then listen to the conversation and choose the correct answer.

1. What are you going to do this weekend?
   A. That sounds nice.
   B. I'm going hiking on Saturday.
   C. He might graduate in June.
   D. Thank you.

2. What are your plans for this week?
   A. I might have some friends over for dinner Tuesday.
   B. That sounds like a nice weekend.
   C. No, thank you.
   D. No, I don't.

3. What is Bob going to do on Friday?
   A. go shopping
   B. go to a movie
   C. do some projects around the house
   D. have some friends over for dinner

4. What is Bob going to do on Saturday?
   A. have some friends over for dinner
   B. do some projects around the house
   C. stay in
   D. go to a movie

5. What is Bob going to do on Sunday?
   A. go shopping
   B. do some projects around the house
   C. have some friends over for dinner
   D. go to a movie

GRAMMAR AND VOCABULARY: Choose the correct word or phrase to complete each sentence.

6. Sam _____ see a movie this weekend.
   A. is
   B. is going
   C. is going to
   D. going

7. Ann and Amy _____ go to the beach on Saturday.
   A. is going to
   B. are going to
   C. going to
   D. going

8. She _____ have friends over for dinner this weekend.
   A. isn't going to
   B. aren't going to
   C. not go
   D. isn't going

9. When _____ study this weekend?
   A. he going to
   B. be going to
   C. is he going to
   D. is he going

10. Rob and Sara might _____ married next year.
    A. get
    B. gets
    C. getting
    D. will get

11. Nick _____ graduate next June.
    A. will probably
    B. probably
    C. is probably
    D. probably going

12. I _____ have a picnic this Sunday.
    A. doesn't
    B. may not
    C. going
    D. not

13. The opposite of *go out* is _____.
    A. stay up
    B. stay home
    C. stay out
    D. stay over

14. We're going to take it easy this weekend.
    Another word for *take it easy* is _____.
    A. work out
    B. go hiking
    C. stay up
    D. relax

15. A holiday in July is _____.
    A. Father's Day
    B. Mother's Day
    C. Independence Day
    D. Election Day

16. I was born 20 years ago today.
    Today is my _____.
    A. birthday
    B. graduation
    C. anniversary
    D. wedding

READING: Read the article. Then answer the questions.

Great weather ahead—What are your plans?

By Mark Green *Pine Valley News*

PINE VALLEY Last weekend, we had a big storm. It was very rainy. This weekend, we're expecting good weather. It's going to be warm and sunny this weekend. I talked to a few people downtown and asked them about their plans for the weekend. Here's what they said:

Mike B., mail carrier: I don't have to work this Saturday. My family and I are going to go to the beach. We may go to a movie on Saturday night.

Lisa L., teacher: I'm going to stay inside all day. I might work on some projects. I'm going to have some friends over for dinner on Sunday.

Alan W., cook: I have to work all weekend! But I do have Friday night off. On Friday night, my wife and I are going to go dancing. We love to dance.

Ann C., student: I might play tennis with some friends on Saturday, and I'm going to go shopping on Sunday afternoon.

17. Who wrote the article?
    A. Ann
    B. Mike
    C. Mark
    D. Alan

18. What might Mike do?
    A. go to the beach
    B. go to a movie
    C. go dancing
    D. play tennis

19. What does Lisa plan to do?
    A. have friends over for dinner
    B. celebrate a holiday
    C. teach a class
    D. celebrate the last day of class

20. Where does Alan plan to go?
    A. to work
    B. dancing
    C. to a friend's house
    D. shopping

UNIT 12 Personal Goals

LESSON 1

1 MATCH the words to make correct phrases.

<u> f </u> 1. become   a. with a U.S. passport

_____ 2. learn   b. the citizenship interview

_____ 3. fill out   c. of Allegiance

_____ 4. take a citizenship   d. elections

_____ 5. pass   e. my community

_____ 6. pass a background   f. a citizen

_____ 7. take the Oath   g. the naturalization application

_____ 8. vote in   h. test

_____ 9. travel   i. check

_____ 10. volunteer in   j. citizenship requirements

2 WRITE. Complete the sentences. Use the correct form of the verbs in parentheses.

1. Lucia <u> needs to pass </u> (need / pass) a background check.

2. Marco and Roberto _____ (plan / take) the oath of allegiance.

3. You _____ (need / learn) the citizenship requirements.

4. Mari _____ (plan / vote) in elections.

5. Maria _____ (want / travel) with a U.S. passport.

6. I _____ (plan / volunteer) in my community.

7. Katya _____ (need / fill out) the naturalization application.

8. They _____ (want / pass) the citizenship interview.

3 WHAT ABOUT YOU? Write answers to the questions. Write complete sentences.

1. Do you plan to become a citizen? _____

2. Do you need to learn more English? _____

3. Do you want to learn the citizenship requirements? _____

4. Do you plan to vote in elections? _____

5. Do you want to volunteer in your community? _____

6. Do you want to travel with a U.S. passport? _____

LESSON 2

1 **WRITE** questions and answers about the pictures. Use *plan* and *want*.

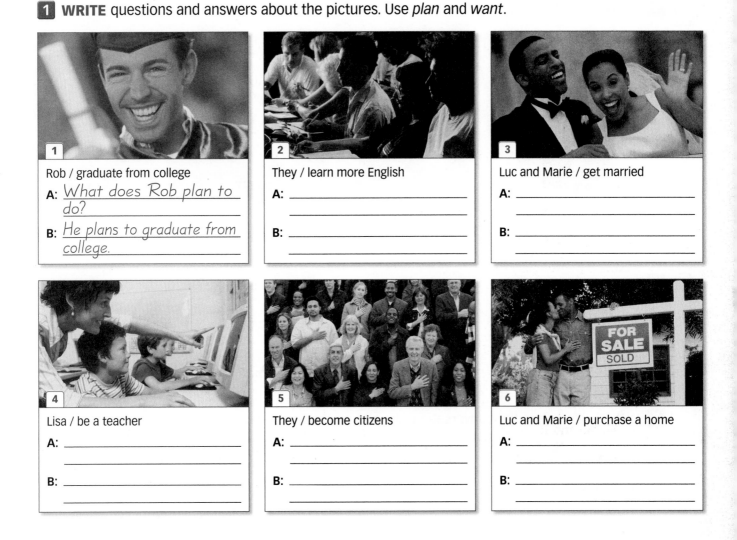

1 Rob / graduate from college
A: *What does Rob plan to do?*
B: *He plans to graduate from college.*

2 They / learn more English
A: _____
_____
B: _____
_____

3 Luc and Marie / get married
A: _____
_____
B: _____
_____

4 Lisa / be a teacher
A: _____
_____
B: _____
_____

5 They / become citizens
A: _____
_____
B: _____
_____

6 Luc and Marie / purchase a home
A: _____
_____
B: _____
_____

2 **WRITE.** Complete the paragraph with the correct form of *want, need,* or *plan* and a verb from the box. There may be more than one correct answer.

be	become	get	get married
go	have	learn	purchase

Ann has a lot of plans and goals. She (1) _____*wants to be*_____ a pharmacist. First, she

(2) _____ more English. Then she (3) _____ a U.S. citizen. After

that, she (4) _____ to college. After she graduates, she (5) _____

a good job, and Bao and she (6) _____ . They (7) _____ a house, and they

also (8) _____ children.

LESSON 3

1 LISTEN and number the pictures.

2 LISTEN to the question. Then listen to the conversation. Fill in the circle for the correct answer.

1. Ⓐ   Ⓑ   Ⓒ

2. Ⓐ   Ⓑ   Ⓒ

3. Ⓐ   Ⓑ   Ⓒ

3 WRITE. Complete the conversation. Use the words and phrases in the box.

a pharmacist	finish my English classes	goal
plan to do	step	to college

A: What is your _____ ?

B: I want to be _____ .

A: What is your first _____ ?

B: First, I need to _____ .

A: What do you _____ after that?

B: Next, I plan to go _____ .

A: That sounds like a good plan. Good luck!

Culture and Communication—*Expressing Congratulations and Good Wishes*

W CD, 61

1 **LISTEN AND READ** the conversations. Then practice them with a partner.

> *Mary:* Hi, Lisa. What's your son doing these days?
>
> *Lisa:* Oh, he's in college. In fact, he plans to graduate this June.
>
> *Mary:* That's wonderful! You must be very proud of him!

> *Alan:* Hi, Raul. What's new?
>
> *Raul:* Oh, I'm going to take the citizenship test tomorrow.
>
> *Alan:* That's great, Raul. Good luck!

2 **WRITE.** Complete the conversations. Use expressions from the box.

Useful Expressions
Expressing Congratulations and Good Wishes

Congratulations!	Good luck.
I'm very happy for you.	Best of luck!
That's wonderful!	You must be very proud . . .
Good for you!	

1. *A:* I got a job today!

   B: _____

   _____.

2. *A:* We're going to get married!

   B: _____.

3. *A:* I passed the citizenship test!

   B: _____.

4. *A:* I plan to move to California next month.

   B: _____.

3 **WRITE.** Think of a happy situation for family members or friends. Write a conversaton. Express congratulations or good wishes. Then practice your conversations with a partner.

A: _____

B: _____

A: _____

B: _____

LESSON 4

1 **MATCH** the picture and the sentence. Then <u>underline</u> the verbs and (circle) the time expressions.

a b c d e

_____ 1. José will be very happy at his graduation in June.

_____ 2. Last year, I earned a certificate of completion.

_____ 3. Sam is going to apply for a student loan next month.

_____ 4. Today, Jane is researching career requirements on the Internet.

_____ 5. Right now, Dave is saving money for college tuition.

2 **CIRCLE** the correct verbs.

1. Sara **graduated / is going to graduate** from college next June.

2. Someday, Mark **will be / was** very proud of his success.

3. Right now, Tom **is saving / saved** money for college.

4. Amy and Rob **got / are getting** married last year.

5. Raul **will become / became** a citizen two years ago.

6. Nick **is going to fill out / filled out** the application tomorrow.

7. Jake **will pay back / paid back** the money after he gets a job.

3 **WRITE.** Unscramble the questions.

1. on / Tuesday / do / What / you / do / mornings / ?

   _____

2. now / you / doing / right / What / are / ?

   _____

3. here / When / come / you / did / ?

   _____

4. years / five / live / ago / Where / you / did / ?

   _____

5. weekend / do / What / going / you / are / to / this / ?

   _____

LESSON 5

1 WRITE answers to the questions in Activity 3.

1. _____
2. _____
3. _____
4. _____
5. _____

WCD, 62

2 LISTEN. Circle the words you hear.

1. I'll   We'll
2. He'll   She'll
3. I'll   You'll
4. I'll   It'll
5. I'll   She'll
6. He'll   She'll
7. She'll   We'll
8. It'll   They'll
9. He'll   She'll
10. I'll   We'll

3 WRITE. Read the situations. Do the math and answer the questions.

1. Ann wants to visit her parents in one year. She needs $2,000 for the trip.
   How much does she need to save each month?

   _____

2. Roberto wants to get married in two years. He needs $4,000 for the wedding.
   How much does he need to save each month?

   _____

3. Raul wants to buy a used car in two years. He needs to save $8,000.
   How much money does he need to save each month?

   _____

4. Marta wants to send her son to college in four years. She needs to save $10,000.
   How much money does she need to save each month?

   _____

Family Connection—*Making a Budget*

1 READ Alan and May's budget.

Monthly Income	
Alan's salary	$2,080.00
May's salary	$1,600.00
A. **Total Monthly Income**	$ _____
Monthly Expenses	
Rent	$1,250.00
Food	$500.00
Utilities (electricity and phone/Internet)	$100.00
Car Insurance	$100.00
Gas	$150.00
Other transportation (bus fare and parking)	$35.00
Clothing	$75.00
Household and personal expenses (cleaning products, soap, aspririn, etc.)	$30.00
Entertainment (2 movies per month; one restaurant per month)	$150.00
B. **Emergencies** (for example, medical problems)	$ _____
C. **Total Monthly Expenses**	$ _____
D. **Save Each Month**	$ _____

2 CIRCLE *yes* or *no*.

1. *Income* means money that comes in.	(yes)	no
2. *Expenses* means money that you spend.	yes	no
3. Alan makes $1,600 a month.	yes	no
4. Alan and May pay $500.00 for rent each month.	yes	no
5. An example of a *utility* is electricity.	yes	no
6. Alan and May's total transportation cost is $285 a month.	yes	no
7. An example of a *household expense* is dishwashing soap.	yes	no
8. Alan and May go out a lot each month.	yes	no

3 **WRITE.** Do the math. Write the answers on the lines in Activity 1.

1. How much money do Alan and May make together each month? Add their salaries. Write the answer next to A, on the budget.

2. Alan and May want to have 10 percent of their total monthly income for emergencies. How much money is that? Multiply their total income by 0.10. Write the answer next to B, on the budget.

3. What are Alan and May's total monthly expenses? (Include money for emergencies.) Add all their expenses. Write the number next to C, on the budget.

4. Alan and May plan to purchase a house someday. How much can they save each month to buy a house? Subtract their total expenses from their total income. Write the number next to D, on the budget.

4 **WHAT DO YOU THINK?** Is there any way Alan and May can save more money each month? Write your ideas on the lines.

_____

_____

 5 **WHAT ABOUT YOU?** Make a budget for yourself.

Monthly Income	
Salary	$ _____
Other income	$ _____
Total Monthly Income	$ _____
Monthly Expenses	
Rent	$ _____
Food	$ _____
Utilities	$ _____
Transportation	$ _____
Gas	$ _____
Clothing	$ _____
Household and personal expenses	$ _____
Entertainment	$ _____
Emergencies	$ _____
Other	$ _____
Entertainment	$ _____
Total Monthly Expenses	$ _____
Save Each Month	$ _____

6 **REAL-LIFE LESSON.** Ask family members or friends for advice on saving money. What ideas do they have?

_____

_____

Community Connection—*Evaluating Savings Accounts*

1 MATCH the banking word and the meaning.

__c__	1. balance	a.	the smallest amount
_____	2. deposit	b.	take money out of a bank account
_____	3. interest	c.	the total amount of money in a bank account
_____	4. minimum	d.	money that you put in the bank; also, money that you start a bank account with
_____	5. withdraw	e.	money that banks pay you for the money that you keep with them

2 READ about some types of bank accounts.

> **Two Types of Savings Accounts**
>
> **Regular Savings Account:** You can start or end this account any time. You earn a small amount of interest, and you can add money or withdraw money any time.
>
> **CD (certificate of deposit):** This account lasts for a certain amount of time. It pays more interest. You can't add money to the account or withdraw money during the time period. When you close the account early, you lose some of your interest.

Pine Valley Bank

Savings Accounts

A Regular Savings: 1.0%; minimum balance: $500.00

B 1-year CD: 4.9%; minimum deposit: $5,000

West Bank

Savings Accounts

C Regular Savings: .95%; no minimum balance

D 5-year CD: 5.2%; $10,000 minimum deposit

East Bank

Savings Accounts

E 1-year CD: 3.9%; $1,000 minimum deposit

F 3-year CD: 5.0%; $5,000 minimum deposit

Countrywide Bank

Savings Accounts

G 3-year CD: 4.9%; $1,000 minimum deposit

H 5-year CD: 5.1%; $5,000 minimum deposit

3 CIRCLE *yes* or *no*.

1. Pine Valley Bank gives the highest interest on regular savings accounts.	(yes)	no
2. Pine Valley Bank and East Bank both have 1-year CD accounts.	yes	no
3. West Bank has the highest interest on a 5-year CD account.	yes	no
4. You need $10,000 to start a 5-year CD account at West Bank.	yes	no
5. Pine Valley Bank has the highest interest on a 1-year CD account.	yes	no
6. You need $3,000 to start a 1-year CD account at East Bank.	yes	no

4 WRITE. Look at the accounts in Activity 2. Find the best savings account for these people. Write the letter of the account on the line.

1. Alan and May have $1,000. They want the highest interest. They don't plan to add or take money out of the account. _____

2. Sam and Liz have $100 to open a savings account. They want to add about $20 to the account each month. _____

3. Wei and Sue have $5,000. They want a CD for the shortest amount of time. They want it for the highest interest. _____

4. Jane wants a CD account. She wants an account with a high interest, and she wants it for the longest amount of time. She has about $6,000, so she wants a low minimum deposit. _____

5. Eric has $500 to open an account. He wants to save for a car. He plans to add $10 each week. _____

5 REAL-LIFE LESSON. Get information on savings accounts and CDs at a bank in your community. Write the information in the chart.

Name of Bank:				
	Interest	Minimum Balance or Deposit	Length of Account (for CDs)	Other Information
Savings Accounts				
CD Accounts				

Career Connection—*Planning a Potluck Picnic*

1 READ. Oscar is planning a picnic for Memorial Day. Read the conversation.

Oscar:	Hi, Eric. I'm planning a picnic at the park for Memorial Day. I want to invite everyone from work.
Eric:	That sounds great! But don't we have to work?
Oscar:	No. Memorial Day is a holiday. It's the Monday after next.
Eric:	Oh, that's perfect! What about the food?
Oscar:	It's going to be a potluck picnic.
Eric:	Oh, so everyone has to bring something. What should I bring?
Oscar:	I'm going to ask everyone to bring a main dish or a salad.
Eric:	I'll make my famous pasta dish.
Oscar:	Great!
Eric:	What about drinks?
Oscar:	I'll bring sodas, and Alfonso's bringing a cake.
Eric:	Okay. Sounds like fun!
Oscar:	Can you help me tell everyone about the picnic?
Eric:	Sure. I'll tell Sofia, and she can tell everyone at the meeting tomorrow.

2 CIRCLE the correct word.

1. The picnic is for **Independence Day /** (**Memorial Day**)

2. The picnic will be on **Sunday / Monday**.

3. The picnic will be at **work / the park**.

4. Alfonso is bringing a **pasta dish / cake**.

5. Oscar is bringing **drinks / a main dish**.

6. Eric is bringing a **main dish / cake**.

3 WRITE answers to the questions.

1. Why can they have the picnic on Monday? _____

2. What does *potluck* mean? _____

3. How will everyone know about the picnic? _____

Technology Connection: Online Bill Paying

WRITE. Look at the computer screen. Oscar is paying bills online. Answer the questions.

---

www.pinevalleybank.com

PINE VALLEY BANK ONLINE BANKING

search the site [GO]

Welcome Oscar Sanchez!

log out

| Home | Accounts | Online Bill Pay | Customer Service |

Online Bill Paying

Account Balance: **$845.30**

Payee	Amount	Pay Date
Electric Company	$35.56	May 15
Phone Bill	$50.71	May 18
Credit Card	$225.34	May 29

(Submit)

---

1. What is the name of Oscar's bank? _____

2. How many bills is Oscar paying? _____

3. What types of bills is he paying? _____

4. How much is Oscar paying for his phone bill? _____

5. What is the pay date for the credit card bill? _____

6. How much does Oscar have in his account? _____

7. What is the total amount of all his bills? _____

Practice Test

LISTENING: Choose the best response. Then listen to the conversation and choose the correct answer.

1. What is your goal?
   A. Good luck!
   B. I plan to become a citizen.
   C. I attend classes on Tuesday mornings.
   D. Yes, I do.

2. What do you plan to do after that?
   A. Next, I plan to go to college.
   B. Yes, I did. I earned a GED certificate.
   C. First, I need to finish my English classes.
   D. No, I didn't.

3. What is the man's goal?
   A. to be a car mechanic
   B. to be a teacher
   C. to be a pharmacist
   D. to be a student

4. What is the man's first step?
   A. to get a job-training certificate
   B. to complete the GED
   C. to learn to drive
   D. to finish his English classes

5. What is the man's next step?
   A. to get a job-training certificate
   B. to finish his English classes
   C. to complete the GED
   D. to get a driver's license

GRAMMAR AND VOCABULARY: Choose the correct word or phrase to complete each sentence.

6. I _____ vote in elections.
   A. plans to
   B. plan
   C. plan to
   D. am planning

7. Ana _____ become a citizen.
   A. wants to
   B. want to
   C. want
   D. wants

8. She _____ to learn more English.
   A. don't need
   B. not need
   C. doesn't need
   D. doesn't

9. He _____ money right now.
   A. saving
   B. is saving
   C. saved
   D. save

10. Nick and Sofia _____ married last year.
    A. will get
    B. gets
    C. are getting
    D. got

11. I _____ a good job after I graduate.
    A. get
    B. is getting
    C. got
    D. will get

12. Why _____ getting a GED?
    A. does you
    B. did you
    C. are you
    D. going to

13. When _____ graduate from college?
    A. does you
    B. did you
    C. are you
    D. going to

14. For my new job, I need to pass _____ .
    A. a passport
    B. a background check
    C. an oath of allegiance
    D. an election

15. Sara is going to find out about getting money for college. Another word for *find out about* is _____ .
    A. reach
    B. graduate
    C. research
    D. complete

16. I borrowed money to go to school. I will _____ the money after I graduate.
    A. pay back
    B. fill out
    C. volunteer
    D. reach

READING: Read the article. Then answer the questions.

Local Immigrant Reaches Goal

Costa Verde, CA—When Anya Petrova was a little girl, she dreamed about becoming a nurse. She grew up in a small village in Russia, and her family was very poor. When Anya was 8, her mother and two younger brothers moved to the United States. In the beginning, their life was very difficult. Anya's mother worked as a seamstress, and they didn't have very much money. Anya had a goal: she wanted to get a good job and take care of her family. First, she learned English. She studied very hard. Then she got a part-time job and attended Costa Verde Community College. Next week, Anya will get her nursing certificate. She hopes to get a job at Costa Verde Hospital. Anya is very excited about her future. Now she will help her family. She is very proud of her success.

17. What is the article about?
    A. moving to the United States
    B. learning English
    C. working part-time
    D. reaching a goal

18. What steps did Anya complete in the past to reach her goal?
    A. learn English and study hard
    B. graduate from community college
    C. help her family
    D. become a nurse

19. What is Anya's goal?
    A. to become a seamstress
    B. to become a nurse
    C. to learn English
    D. to attend community college

20. What are Anya's future steps?
    A. move to the United States and learn English
    B. learn English, study hard, and go to community college
    C. graduate, get a job, and help her family
    D. move to the United States and get a job as a seamstress

Correlation Table

Student Book	Workbook
Pre-Unit	
2–5	2–5
Unit 1	
6–7	6
8–9	7
10–11	8–9
12–13	10
14–15	11
16–17	12–13
18–19	14–15
20	16–17
21	18–19
Unit 2	
22–23	20
24–25	21
26–27	22–23
28–29	24
30–31	25
32–33	26–27
34–35	28–29
36	30–31
37	32–33
Unit 3	
38–39	34
40–41	35
42–43	36–37
44–45	38
46–47	39
48–49	40–41
50–51	42–43
52	44–45
53	46–47
Unit 4	
54–55	48
56–57	49
58–59	50–51
60–61	52
62–63	53
64–65	54–55
66–67	56–57
68	58–59
69	60–61

Student Book	Workbook
Unit 5	
70–71	62
72–73	63
74–75	64–65
76–77	66
78–79	67
80–81	68–69
82–83	70–71
84	72–73
85	74–75
Unit 6	
86–87	76
88–89	77
90–91	78–79
92–93	80
94–95	81
96–97	82–83
98–99	84–85
100	86–87
101	88–89
Unit 7	
102–103	90
104–105	91
106–107	92–93
108–109	94
110–111	95
112–113	96–97
114–115	98–99
116	100–101
117	102–103
Unit 8	
118–119	104
120–121	105
122–123	106–107
124–125	108
126–127	109
128–129	110–111
130–131	112–113
132	114–115
133	116–117

Student Book	Workbook
Unit 9	
134–135	118
136–137	119
138–139	120–121
140–141	122
142–143	123
144–145	124–125
146–147	126–127
148	128–129
149	130–131
Unit 10	
150–151	132
152–153	133
154–155	134–135
156–157	136
158–159	137
160–161	138–139
162–163	140–141
164	142–143
165	144–145
Unit 11	
166–167	146
168–169	147
170–171	148–149
172–173	150
174–175	151
176–177	152–153
178–179	154–155
180	156–157
181	158–159
Unit 12	
182–183	160
184–185	161
186–187	162–163
188–189	164
190–191	165
192–193	166–167
194–195	168–169
196	170–171
197	172–173